IMPARTING *REVIVAL FIRE*
Through America's Young Generation

---

by

Sandy Davis Kirk, Ph.D.

McDougal Publishing is a ministry of The McDougal Foundation, Inc., a Maryland nonprofit corporation dedicated to spreading the Gospel of the Lord Jesus Christ to as many people as possible in the shortest time possible.

Published by:

McDougal Publishing
P.O. Box 3595
Hagerstown, MD   21742-3595
www.mcdougalpublishing.com

ISBN 1-58158-053-3

Printed in the United States of America
For Worldwide Distribution

Dedication

You wash my feet with your tears and humble my heart with your passion. You fill the air with your cries for revival and burn the atmosphere with your thirst after God. You are the future Steve Hills and Benny Hinns of this nation. To you, our camp ministry team — Jon, Ariel, Daniel, Duane, Jared, Jonathan, David, Matt, Curt, Tim, and Fabienne — I dedicate this book.

Acknowledgments

No one writes a book alone. Along the way, God uses special people to help shape the message. My deepest gratitude goes to the young men who grace our ministry team, whose stories I tell in these pages, and who have listened and responded as I've read them these chapters.

Further gratitude fills me when I think of my former pastor, Glen Swartzendruber, and his family, as well as our home church in Idalou, Texas. You encouraged me and helped me start a revival camp in the Pensacola area, and out of this experience came the story of this book.

Now, here at Brownsville, the people have fully opened their hearts to me. When they saw my sincere love for the young generation, they knew my motives were real. I thank my friends Valerie and Joe Civelli and Jerry and Heli Pilgrim for first believing in my vision from the Lord. I thank Dr. Larry Martin for inviting me to teach at the school of ministry. I especially thank my hero, Pastor Richard Crisco, for seeing my heart and encouraging me along the way. All who know you thank God for your sincere love and tears and your willingness to worship unashamedly before the Lord.

Special thanks also to our beloved Pastor John Kilpatrick, who leads and tenderly pastors this remarkable revival. It is an indescribable privilege to be part of what God is doing in this seaside city on the Gulf Coast. As David Yonggi Cho, pastor of the world's largest congregation, prophesied, "I am going to send revival to the seaside city of Pensacola, and it will spread like a fire until all of America has been consumed by it."[1]

Endnote:

1. David Yonggi Cho, "Foreword," *Feast of Fire* (Pensacola: John Kilpatrick, 1995), p. vii.

Contents

Foreword by Pastor Richard Crisco

I will never forget the couple of years just before the Brownsville Revival got started. I had become extremely frustrated with youth ministry. I was fasting, praying, and preaching as hard as I knew how, and yet I was not seeing the results I felt I should be seeing. I was actually ready to quit youth ministry. Then one morning, during my devotions, the Lord dropped a scripture into my spirit. I had never had that experience before, and it has never happened since in quite that same way. The passage of scripture He impressed upon me that day was Psalm 24:6. It says, *"This is the generation of them that seek him, that seek thy face, O Jacob. Selah"* (KJV).

The Lord told me to hang on because I was about to experience a generation that was sick and tired of dead religion and wanted nothing less than His Presence. The current generation had sought His hand, seeing what they could get from Him. But God said He was in the process of raising up a generation that would not be interested just in what He could do for them. They would desire to know Him face to face! And it happened. Over the past several years at Brownsville I have witnessed firsthand a radical generation that is hungry for nothing less than the awesome presence of God.

The Lord showed me that He wanted to restore three things back to the Church through this generation —

9

worship, intercession, and the prophetic, and He is doing it. Over the last few years, I have experienced the most powerful prayer meetings ever, as hundreds of teenagers and young adults fervently cry out to the Lord in intercession for hours. This is the greatest time to be in youth ministry, because the Lord is raising up a generation of spiritual giants, warriors who will sweep across the nations with a bold proclamation of the Gospel.

The Church does not need more professional pastors or political preachers, but we need some praying prophets who will stand in the pulpits and deliver a "Thus saith the Lord!" The Lord is searching for some Elijahs, prophets of fire, who will pour their heart and soul into this younger Elisha generation. Dr. Sandy Kirk is one of those prophetic voices who has a passion for the presence of God and has devoted her life to this unique generation.

As you read the stories and accounts captured within the pages of this book, may your own heart be set ablaze with the burning passion to know the Lord in a more intimate manner. The Lord is setting *America Ablaze* with His Spirit once again, and the fact that you are even reading these opening statements causes me to believe that you, too, will be a vital part of this last-time revival. Till Jesus comes, let us burn with a passion for Him!

Pastor Richard Crisco
Youth Pastor, Brownsville Assembly of God
Interim President, BRSM
(Brownsville Revival School of Ministry)

Introduction

I doubled over in tears one night in 1996 in the midst of a revival at Harvest Rock Church in Pasadena, California. For more than a year I had been soaking in the streams of this refreshing renewal. Then, suddenly, the Holy Spirit poured the pain of your generation down upon me. I wept and wept in deep intercession. It was as though the hand of God reached in, gripped my heart, and squeezed it. I could actually feel the pain God experiences over the wounds of your generation.

With so many shattered homes and absent fathers, your generation has become known as "the fatherless generation." I believe God's heart aches over the pain this causes you. I know He filled my heart with His burden for you and your generation.

As soon as I finished seminary in California, I returned home to Texas. There, at my home church, the Lord gave me a vision of *America Ablaze* with revival. Flashing before the eyes of my spirit, I saw a map of the United States with an American flag waving through it. The words *"America Ablaze"* streaked across the map, and flames of fire burned all around the edges. The Holy Spirit said, "I am setting *America Ablaze* with revival, and you can be part of it — if you'll let Me lead you."

Compelled by this vision and by the heavy burden for your generation, I moved to the Pensacola, Florida, area to start a revival camp. I had visited revivals all over the nation as I did my research, but what I now witnessed at Brownsville took my breath away. I saw the power of God burning down on a young generation. I watched hundreds of young men and women explod ing with passion for Jesus and a burden for souls. In response, I started a revival camp, naming it (because of the vision the Lord had given me) "Camp America Ablaze."

Now I invite you to come through the pages of this book to see revival students ministering to a young generation. Come see young hearts thunder with passion. Watch the tears roll from their eyes as they worship, and see them literally vibrating under the power of God's presence. See "nameless, faceless" young men and women pray for each other and feel the power of revival streaming down upon you.

As you read, I pray you will breathe in a fresh breath of revival. Breathing in revival is like inhaling the atmosphere of Heaven. It will refresh you, heal your pain, and cause the life of God to flow through you.

Even as America shakes, something amazing burns in the soul of your generation. Though dread of war and blows of terrorism strike fear in the hearts of many, you are called by God to start fires of revival throughout the land. I believe you were born for revival, destined to be "spiritual arsonists," as Winkie Pratney, a man who has given his life to minister to your generation, has so aptly said.[1]

Bill Bright, the founder of Campus Crusade for Christ, received a word from the Lord in 1994. Rushing in to tell his wife, he exclaimed, "North America and much of the world will, before the end of the year 2000, experience a great spiritual awakening!" He continued, "And this revival will spark the greatest spiritual harvest in the history of the Church."[2] That revival, like an underground fire, already quietly burns in the hearts of the young.

If you yearn to catch these holy sparks, come join me now in the pages of this book. Come see how God has heard your cry and is pouring revival down upon a wounded generation. Come receive a fresh revelation of the Lamb and discover how you can have a part in setting *America Ablaze.*

Sandy Kirk
Pensacola, Florida

Endnotes:

1. Winkie Pratney, "Foreword" to Charles Finney's *Crystal Christianity*, David L. Young, ed. (Pittsburgh: Whitaker House, 1985), p. 5.
2. Bill Bright, *The Coming Revival: America's Call to Fast, Pray and "Seek God's Face"* (Orlando, FL: New Life Publications, 1995), pp. 35-36.

He will come like a pent-up flood that the breath of the LORD *drives along.*　　　　Isaiah 59:19

The Cry That Pierced God's Heart

A Young Man's Cry

Chapter 1

The Cry That Pierced God's Heart

One night, at a high point of worship at the Brownsville Revival, where the waters of revival run deep, the Holy Spirit said to me:

> I have dripped tears over the wounds in the soul of America. I've wept over the injustices and the blood that soaked into the ground of the nation. I've heard the cries of the poor, the lost, and the broken ones. But there is a cry of all cries. As I've looked down on planet earth, I have heard the cry of a fatherless generation, and *their cry has pierced My heart.*

The Lord showed me this cry, on one level, as "Daddy, where are You? Why have You forsaken me?" On a deeper level, the cry is, "My God, why have even You forsaken me?"

I believe this is why God has chosen your generation for revival. Your cry has pierced His heart and opened the fountain of revival upon you.

You may be wondering, however, just what revival is. Robert Coleman, director of the Billy Graham Center for Evangelism at Wheaton College, said, "Revival is breathing in the breath of God."[1] D. Martyn Lloyd-Jones, considered by some the greatest preacher of the twentieth century, said that revival is "God coming down."[2]

I believe this is why revival is God's divine answer for the pain of your generation. When you breathe in the breath of God, the holes in your heart fill with life, His life. The ache inside soothes and washes away, and fresh hope, passion, and purpose spring up within you.

The Pain of a Generation

We could survey America's history from the dawn of the nation to the sunrise of the twenty-first century, and never would we find a more wounded generation than yours. If you don't carry a father-wound, from abandonment by your dad, you can be sure that most of your friends do.

With over half of your families splintered and scattered by divorce, many of you grew up as the first latchkey kids in American history. The effects of abuse, abandonment, and rejection can be seen in the rising rates of drug, alcohol, and sexual addictions. Pandemic rates of sexually transmitted diseases, soaring numbers of suicides,[3] and massacres in schools are related to the wounds of a fatherless group of young men and women. Yours is a grief-torn and angry generation.

Richard Crisco, president of Brownsville Revival School of Ministry and youth pastor at Brownsville, said, "This generation is the most abused, neglected, and misunderstood generation in the history of mankind. Hopelessness has gripped their hearts."[4]

Brownsville's campus youth pastor, Donny Lewis, told me, "These kids don't know which end is up. Mom has them in the winter and blasts Dad; Dad has them in the summer and blasts Mom. They're in situations of incest, illegitimacy, and abuse, and when we first see them here at the revival, many of them are on the verge of suicide."[5]

Youth pastor Tim Conder said, "I continually confront the crisis of teen depression, preoccupation with death, suicidal impulses, and families in which a teen suicide has occurred."[6]

Though the popular media sometimes try to depict the married, two-parent family as a source of pathology, the truth is—the breakup of your family has probably ripped your world apart.[7]

Kevin Ford, nephew of Billy Graham, speaking for your generation, said, "Many of us are bitter and calloused over having been neglected or abused in dysfunctional families. We are confused, sad, angry, and clinically depressed. ... For generation X,[8] the past is forever beyond reach, the present is black and bleak, and the future is a brick wall."[9] Ford concludes:

We are, as a generation, bitter toward our parents for divorcing at a rate two or three times higher than our grandparents.[10] They didn't consider how we would feel when divorce tore our entire world apart. They didn't think about how kids tend to internalize and take on the blame and shame for their parents' problems. *Kids are resilient*, they thought. *They'll get over it.* Yeah, right.[11]

Young man or woman reading these pages, I know it's hard to forgive, but would you allow me to say something to you right now? Please understand that these words come from the depths of my heart.

I, too, have experienced the pain of rejection and physical abuse — not from an abusive or neglectful father, but from a man I loved. So I think I know how you feel. Most of all, I have felt God's pain over the ache in the soul of your generation, and I want to ask your forgiveness.

Repenting to Your Generation

Right now, young man, young woman, I want to kneel down and take you by the hand. I want to look right into your eyes and, with all the sincerity of my heart, say to you—I am so sorry. We were wrong.

I am sorry for the divorce. I know it tore your heart to pieces. I know you cried yourself to sleep at night and withdrew from your parents because of the pain.

Maybe the pain became so severe that you tried to find relief in drugs, or alcohol, or sex, or gangs, or maybe even in a suicide attempt.

I say to you, I am so sorry for the way you had to come home to an empty house because your mom was working so hard just to keep the bills paid. I am so sorry for the aloneness you felt. The ache of loneliness hurt deeply. I am terribly sorry.

Because your parents may not be able to say this to you yet, please allow me to say what you need to hear. I hurt for the way you blamed yourself. It was not your fault, but you thought—*If only I could have been better, Dad wouldn't have left.* This is a lie, but it has probably tormented you through the years.

You must allow the truth to set you free, for you are completely innocent. This is an adult problem, perhaps the result of a father-wound in your own dad. I'll say more about this "father-wound" later, but for now, please believe me—the divorce was not your fault in any way.

I am heartsick about the shame you suffered when your parents divorced. It made you feel worthless and rejected and without an identity. You buried the grief and have carried it all these years.

I think it must feel like a knife dipped in poison, still stabbing you in the heart. If somehow I could reach in and dislodge the knife of pain, I would. I can't, but please allow me to just tell you how deeply sorry I am. I want you to know that I do understand your hurt, and I weep with you.

And, if you are feeling some tears rise up right now, I urge you to let them flow. Let the rivers of grief come streaming out. Don't dam them up or choke them back.

God wants you to cleanse the riverbeds of your soul, so He can fill you back up with His river of revival. But first, in the presence of Jesus, let the tears of grief and rage roll out.

If I were there with you, I would give you my shoulder and say, "Please, cry on me, like a child in a mother's arms." I'm not there in person, but God is. Let the Comforter come right now—the Holy Spirit Himself—and let Him help you release the pent-up pain.

It's like the story of the little boy who heard that his neighbor's wife had died. Suddenly, he rushed to his neighbor's house and hopped up in his lap. Later, his mother asked, "What did you say to him?" "Nothing," the little boy said. "I just helped him cry."[12]

If you will cry with the Holy Spirit until the tears subside, you can expect the healing to begin. So, if you have begun to let the grief out, now I'm asking you to forgive. Let me stand in the gap for your mom or dad, and say, "We were so wrong. Will you please forgive me? Forgive us?"

And will you forgive yourself? In fact, if this applies, right now go look in a mirror and say to yourself, "I am not to blame." Look into your own eyes and say, "It was not my fault. I forgive myself." Say your own name: "_____ , I forgive you."

Now, you can ask Jesus to give you the power to forgive. Only when you let Him wash out all the bitterness toward your parents can you be set free. Only when you let Him cleanse you of the anger can you receive all He has to give you.

You see, God has heard your cry. It has pierced His heart and opened up the floodgates of Heaven. He has a heavenly river to pour down upon you. It's a torrent of His presence and power with which to fill the hole in your soul.

That's why I've written this book, and this is why I want to take you inside scenes of revival in your generation. I want to encourage you, inspire you, and give you hope.

In these pages, you'll see young men and women, just like yourself, with tears wetting their cheeks. They are tears of release for their pent-up grief, and also tears of repentance and cleansing. But you will see these tears transformed to tears of extravagant joy.

And you'll know this is real. I know you hate hypocrisy and sham and religious manipulation. You can't tolerate anything that's not authentic. But when you feel the fire burning down upon you, when your heart races and glows with the heat of revival, when joy bubbles up from within you—you'll know this is real.

Furthermore, when you see those in your own generation bursting with passion for Jesus, their passion will ignite something in you. Hope will kindle and burn until passion flames in you, too.

You'll know God has seen your brokenness and singled you out for a special purpose. He calls you into rivers of revival which spill from His pierced and opened heart.

You see, no cry moves God more deeply. The reason is that He has heard this cry before. He heard it on a warm spring day two thousand years ago.

The Cry of the Son

So, come with me now to a sun-drenched hill just outside Jerusalem. Slip up close to the middle cross and stand with open heart. Look up at God the Son dangling between Heaven and earth on two blood-soaked strips of wood. See the sky blacken. Hear the thunder boom. Watch the lightning sizzle across the heavens.

Open wide your heart and feel what God felt as He looked down on His only Son. Look beyond the mocking multitude and weeping women. See past the blood dripping from every wound, the muscles convulsing, and the nerves screaming in pain. View beyond the shame of nakedness and the suffering of gradual suffocation.

Imagine the agony, the shame, and the grief Jesus felt in that moment, but look deeper. Lift your vision higher. Even look past the horror of human sin bursting down upon Him. Look now, and see into the Father's cup.

Gaze in awe as the Father tips the cup over His Son. Behold the gruesome contents spilling down upon the Innocent One. This was the cup Jesus cried about in Gethsemane. So horrible were the ingredients of this cup that He fell with His face to the ground, writhing in agony in pools of bloody sweat.

Watch now, as the Father, with trembling heart, turns His face of love away from His beloved Son and spills down upon Him the contents of the cup. See wave after wave of punishment for your sin burn like leaping flames against the innocent Lamb. See Jesus become the burnt offering, called the holocaust offering in the Old Testament, for He is God's holocaust. See Him punished for your iniquity, smitten and afflicted and crushed by God His Father (see Isaiah 53:4-5).

Had you realized that He loves you so much? Jesus loves you so deeply and wants to have you near Him so badly that He was willing to take all the punishment for your sins and suffer Hell for you.

Finally, when He can bear the punishment no longer, He pushes down on the nail in His feet to lift His lungs and take in a deep breath of air. Then He roars (it is not a whisper, but a deep, guttural, animal-like roar): *"Eli, Eli, lama sabachthani? ... My God, my God, why hast thou forsaken me?"* (Matthew 27:46, KJV).

Do you see? This was your cry! Your generation was so precious to the Father that He sent His only Son to the cross to cry your heart cry. Jesus wailed the cry of your heart from the cross so that you would never, never, never be forsaken by your God.

Do you realize what this means? All those tears you soaked into your pillow at night when the lights were off and the door was closed ... all those muffled sobs you thought God never heard ... all the times you silently wailed, "My God, where are You? Why have even You forsaken me?" He heard your cry. He saw every tear. He felt every convulsion of pain within you.

That's why—there, on two bloody stakes of wood—Jesus wept your tears. He drank your cup. He shrieked the silent scream of your soul so that, now, He can run to the sound of your cry:

25

> *For because He Himself [in His humanity] has*
> *suffered ... , He is able [immediately] to RUN TO*
> *THE CRY of ... those who ... [therefore are being*
> *exposed to suffering].*   Hebrews 2:18, AMP

Yes, many cries rise up to the heart of God, but yours is the cry of all cries. It has released upon you a river of revival, for this is the cry that pierced the heart of God.

Endnotes:

1. Robert Coleman, "What Is Revival?" in *Accounts of a Campus Revival, Wheaton College 1995,* Timothy Beougher and Lyle Dorsett, eds. (Wheaton, IL: Harold Shaw Publishers, 1995), p.14.
2. D. Martyn Lloyd-Jones, *Revival* (Wheaton, IL: Crossway Books, 1986, pp. 305-306).
3. George Barna, president of the Barna Research Institute, notes that since 1950, suicide rates have tripled for those between eighteen and twenty-four (George Barna, *Generation Next: What You Need to Know About Today's Youth* (Ventura, CA: Regal Books, 1995), p.24.
   Stephen Arterburn and Jim Burns, in *When Love Is Not Enough*, observed that while twenty-seven percent of all young people in the group which many call "generation X" have attempted suicide, a whopping seventy-three percent have actually considered it. Arterburn and Burns point out that among those who have attempted suicide, they have experienced parental loss before the age of twelve; the parents may be talking about divorce or separation; a history of depression exists within the family; a parent was chronically ill during the young person's adolescence; the child has been sexually or physically abused (Stephen Arterburn and Jim Burns, *When Love Is Not Enough* (Colorado Springs, CO: Focus on the Family Publishing, 1992), p.10.
   The term "generation X" actually came from a novel written by one of your generation—Douglas Coupland—entitled *Generation X: Tales of an Accelerated Culture*. To Coupland's dismay, the label stuck. Reacting to this demeaning title, Kevin Ford wrote, "Thanks, but no thanks, Doug. Sounds too much like 'Brand X.' There is a blankness, a lack of identity, even a sense of negation in that big letter X that is disturbing to our self-image" (Kevin Ford, 1995, p.18).
4. Richard Crisco, *It's Time: Passing Revival to the Next Generation* (Shippensburg, PA: Revival Press, 1997), p. x.
5. Personal interview with Donny Lewis at Brownsville Assembly of God, Pensacola, FL, 1999.
6. Kevin Graham Ford, *Jesus for a New Generation: Putting the Gospel in the Language of Xers* (Downers Grove, IL: InterVarsity Press, 1995), p. 18.
7. The primary emotion experienced by children of divorce is deep grief. Along with grief, the children lose their sense of identity. They are plagued with feelings of guilt, tending to blame themselves for their parents' divorce (Dave

Bailey and Leo Carney, *Hope for Dead-End Kids* [Shippensburg, PA:Destiny Image Publishers, 1994], pp. 63-65).

Strauss and Howe report that in 1962 half of all American women believed parents should stay in a bad marriage for the sake of the children. By 1980 only twenty percent thought this. Thus, by 1980, young people faced twice the risk of family breakup as their boomer parents faced and three times the risk of the former generation, called the "builders" or "silents." Most divorced parents today confess to being happier, but they are exacting a heavy toll in the pain and dysfunction of their own children (William Strauss and Neil Howe, *Generations: The History of America's Future* [New York: William Morrow Publishers, 1991], p. 325).

8. I apologize for using the term "generation X," which I consider an insulting tag with a rather hollow and harsh ring. This is the sociological name given to those born between 1965 and 1983, but I only use it when I'm quoting others.

9. Kevin Ford, *Jesus for a New Generation*, pp. 25, 27.

10. It is also true that this generation is the most aborted generation in American history. They admit to feeling unwanted and in the way of their boomer parents' dream for success. They bitterly resent being pushed aside for parents' ambitions or addictions. "Sure we're alienated," sneered an American university student, "but who wouldn't be, in our shoes?" (quoted in Strauss and Howe, *Generations*, p. 330).

11. Kevin Ford, *Jesus for a New Generation*, p. 47.

Clinical psychologist James Osterhaus wrote the following about the pain of divorce in his book *Family Ties Don't Have to Bind*: "We used to think that divorce had only a short-term effect on children—they feel some sadness, some anger, but eventually they get used to the idea and bounce back. Now we know the old adage 'Kids are resilient' was a lot of bilge. The effects of divorce are long-lasting—in some ways lifelong. For most children of divorce, that event represented the disintegration of the child's entire world and sense of security. It was the defining moment in that person's life" (James Osterhaus, *Family Ties Don't Have to Bind* [Nashville, TN: Thomas Nelson Publishers, 1994], p. 20).

12. Jack Canfield and Mark Victor Hansen, *A Third Serving of Chicken Soup for the Soul* (Deerfield Beach, FL: Health Communications, Inc.) 1996, p.12.

Jesus Understands

A River
Rolls Down

A River of Revival

Chapter 2

A River Rolls Down

An eight-year-old boy cringes on the curb in front of his low-income house in Georgia, wiping away tears. Fear grips his heart as his father slams the front door and screeches away in his car. This is the first time he's walked out on his family, but there will be many more times before a final split comes.

The whole world crumbles that day for this little boy. *What will I do now?* he thinks. *I won't have a daddy.* Suddenly it's as though the Holy Spirit surrounds him with the arms of God, soothing away fear and comforting the boy. He whispers to him, "Don't be afraid. I'll take you up and I'll be your Father."[1]

A River for the Fatherless

Years pass, and that little boy becomes a pastor with a passion for revival. At night, he goes to his church and cries to God, sometimes in a fetal position on the front pew, begging God to send revival to his church. With loud wails, he pleads with God for revival, for a visitation from Heaven, for God to breathe down the Holy Spirit in power.

Then one day it happens. God opens Heaven and pours down a river of revival in this man's church. That man is John Kilpatrick, pastor of the Brownsville Assembly of God in Pensacola, the fatherless boy to whom God promised to be a Father.

The revival came on the first Father's Day after the death of Pastor Kilpatrick's mother. It was as if God was saying, "Remember the promise I made to you when you were a little boy? To show you how I keep My promises, receive this!"[2] Then He poured down the longest-running revival in American history. And He did it on Father's Day![3]

But why did God choose Father's Day? I believe the Lord was looking down on a fatherless pastor, weeping for revival. He saw the sincerity of this man's heart, and He wanted to use him and his whole church to touch the world with revival.

But I also believe the fact that God chose Father's Day says something to you. He looked down on a whole generation, many of whom are fatherless. He watched the tears moistening your eyes when you were all alone at night. He felt the hollow ache in your heart. Most of all, He heard your cry, bellowing silently from your brokenness. He wanted you to know He is a *"Father to the fatherless"* (Psalm 10:14 and 18).[4]

So He ran to the sound of your cry. He poured down revival on a fatherless pastor's church in Pensacola, and called you into the healing streams. Though many in my generation have been too preoccupied or fearful to respond, He knew that multitudes from your generation would feel the tugging of His Spirit to come and be revived.

Of course, this isn't the only deep well of revival today. Others, such as Toronto, Pasadena, Kansas City, Tampa, and Baltimore, have been dug around this country. It doesn't matter where; it matters that you come to the river and drink. I personally chose to move near the Brownsville Revival because of the incredible outpouring that was coming here on your generation.

Look Inside ...

Come now inside the Brownsville Revival, and you'll see this river rolling down, not just upon older folks, but profoundly upon the young.

Slip inside the doors and see young men and women exploding in passionate praise and worship. Watch them leaping and dancing like David. Look at the joy bursting from their lips and gleaming in their tears.

See worship leader Lindell Cooley finding the opening in the veil and leading the people into the Holy of Holies. Feel the worship build, and hear the intercessors wailing in the presence of God. See the glory of God burning on every face. You are almost in Heaven, worshiping Jesus Christ face-to-face.

Feel your own heart racing as the presence of the Lord increases. See people around you kneel, then fall on their faces. Watch them weep in humility. Some are crying for sheer joy. Others sob out their pain in the presence of God. Watch them repenting of their sin with shameless abandon. Note the tears openly splashing their cheeks and soaking the carpet.

Stand back and observe as their bodies fall limp, some too weak to move. See others quietly rise and stretch their arms toward Heaven. Even their fingers grasp high, as if to reach up and touch the face of God.

See them open their hearts wide to the presence of God now flooding down upon them. Watch the soft light of holiness shining on their faces. See their tears of sorrow transformed to tears of holy adoration. Observe the beauty of worship in the power and awe of revival.

A Young Generation Worships

When I first entered the sanctuary at the Brownsville Revival, tears blinded me. In fact, such a spirit of repentance came upon me that I broke for two hours, sobbing in repentance over intellectual pride.

I knew that what I was witnessing was true revival because of the great spirit of repentance from sin that was so thick in the air. Charles Finney said:

> In a true revival, Christians are always brought under such conviction; they see their sins in such a light that often they find it impossible to maintain a hope of their acceptance with God. ... There are always, in a genuine revival, deep convictions of sin.[5]

When conviction lifted and my tears finally dried, I

looked around the church. What I saw took my breath away. I saw indescribable passion in the young men and women, and I wondered, *How must God feel when He looks down on this adoring worship from the young?*

I believe His eyes scan worship services throughout the planet, searching. At last He finds what He's longed to see. There she is; there he is.

A nineteen-year-old boy, though empty and rejected by his dad, now stretches his hands as high as he can reach, worshiping, praising, dancing in total abandonment.

A sixteen-year-old girl, though raped and abused, now weeps with delight in the presence of the Lord. She has found the love she's been searching for all of her life.

A twenty-nine-year-old man, tears sloshing down his cheeks, worships with all his heart. Though filled with feelings of worthlessness, now he releases himself to the Lord and finds His worth in Jesus.

God looks down and His heart moves with this adoring worship from the young. Why does this sight so move Him? He's seen worshipers as far back as David and before. But there's something different about this worship. It comes from a fatherless generation.

Revival for the Young

As I witnessed this for the first time, I thought to myself, *This is the clearest example of the power of revival for the young generation I've ever seen. Let the critics storm, but these young adults need a tangible experience with the living presence of God.*

It was clear to me that revival is indeed God's response to the pain of your generation. As Lou Engle said, "The cute little programs won't cut it any more for a generation threatened in the womb, molested in childhood, and desperately crying out for a reason not to die."[6]

The burden of the Lord for this fatherless generation kept mounting and aching in my spirit. As I said earlier, as soon as I finished my seminary work, I pulled up stakes from my home in Texas and moved to the Pensacola area.

Once there, I bought Steve Hill's home, turning it into a "revival camp" for youth and college students. My goal was to help get kids and young adults to the revival, but I also wanted to give revival students the opportunity to impart revival to their generation.

It was here at camp that I began to see the passion even more. Every morning we would walk down to the prayer garden under the oak trees, and there one of the ministry students from the Brownsville Revival School of Ministry would give a gripping testimony.

Stories of Pain and Passion

Their stories broke me. Most of them came from broken homes, with dads who had rejected or abandoned them. Many, out of sheer rage, had become addicted to drugs or alcohol, or had become entrapped by pornography or other sexual addictions.

My heart wept as I heard Anthony tell about his father leaving before he was born. His mother remarried, but when he was thirteen, she died, leaving him with a stepfather who, in drunken rages, beat him.

Another young man told his story of anger. The violent temper of his father, who often exploded in front of him, had deeply affected him. Such hatred toward his dad filled him that he actually identified with the murderous rage of Dylan and Eric at Columbine High School. He said, "If I'd had the nerve, I would have blown up my school, too!"

Another of the young men had been cruelly treated and rejected by his father. As a means of escape, he retreated into pornography and other sexual sin and had developed an out-of-control addiction. A young woman told of being raped and having a child out of wedlock.

Then, one by one, they all told of how Jesus had brought them to the revival and had powerfully touched their lives. He had opened Heaven and poured His power upon their broken places. Every one of them had repented in soul-cleansing godly sorrow. They had wept out their sin in the presence of God, until He had released them from misery and the bondage of sin.

Now I saw them exploding before God in abandoned worship and praise. I had never seen such reckless, extravagant passion for Jesus in older folks—much less in the young. The deeper the crevices of pain in their souls, it seemed, the greater was their passion for the Lord. Then I realized—*He who is forgiven much loves much* (see Luke 7:47).

These young adults had been chained down with drugs, alcohol, sex, hatred, and gangs. Of course, these were only symptoms of the deeper pain—primarily the father-wound of forsakenness and abandonment. But when Jesus forgave their sin and washed it all away, they were overwhelmed with gratitude.

Then, when revival began to fill the carved-out pits in their souls, they "went ballistic" with gratitude. Their joy was boundless, and it exploded out of them in singing, dance, worship, and tears.

Pastor Richard Crisco, whose heart burns with the love of a father for his young people, says that these kids are abused, neglected, and hopeless. "But when they come in contact with Life, they explode. He is the One they have been searching for."[7] The life pouring down on your generation flows from the river of God.

Let's pause for a moment now and look back again to Calvary, to see the first time this river rolled down. Once you see the source of this river, you'll understand why it's for you.

The Divine Rupture

Peer first into the Garden of Gethsemane. See Jesus writhing on the ground in a pool of bloody sweat, pleading with His Father to remove the gruesome cup. *"Abba, Father,"* He cries. *"Everything is possible for you"* (Mark 14:36).

How do you think this made the Father feel? This was His Son who had been with Him through all eternity (see John 1:18). Now, His beloved Son was appealing to Him on the basis of this intimacy. *"Abba Father,"* Jesus calls Him, which is the most intimate name for a father one can give. It means a close and endearing "Daddy." This is the deepest cry of the human heart.

Now, see a Son bleeding in agony on two wooden timbers. Hear Him scream out through the universe, *"My God, My God, why have You forsaken Me?"* The cry soars through the heavens and strikes the heart of Abba Father.

When the eternal Son screamed those words in the face of His Father, something of divine proportions happened. Abba's heart broke, but the heart of the Son broke as well.

Now hear Jesus utter His final words from the cross and see Him release His spirit to His Abba. Then it happens ... The physical heart of Jesus bursts open. A divine eruption occurs, pouring out blood and water (see John 19:34). It is just as the Scriptures have said, *"I am poured out like water ... . My heart is like wax; it is softened [with anguish] and melted down within me"* (Psalm 22:14, AMP). In fact, the Hebrew word translated here as *"melted"* is *mâçaç*, and it means "to liquefy."

Do you see? Jesus didn't die from nails or whip or sword. He didn't die from asphyxiation or blood loss. Jesus died of a ruptured heart. That's why blood and water flowed out separately.[8] The blood was for cleansing, and the water represented the first release of the river of God.

Abba's River

You see, ever since the closing of the Garden of Eden, the river of God had been treasured up in the heart of the Son. He was the storehouse, the wellspring, the reservoir of the river that flows with life.

When His heart ruptured, out poured that glorious river. A soldier had drawn back his sword and plunged it into the side of the Lord, and that thrust had released the treasure within. That's why the soldier's spear had to dig open the Lord's side, for rich treasures must be mined. In Christ are hidden all *"the unending (boundless, fathomless, incalculable, and exhaustless) riches"* of God (Ephesians 3:8, AMP).

When the spear was shoved into the earthen vessel of the Lord, it struck a rich vein, and out rolled Abba's river. It was only a trickle at first, but at Pentecost it then rushed down in a tumbling flood. Since then, this river of life, first released on the cross, has poured down to earth in special seasons of revival.

This is Abba's river, for now Jesus has become your Abba, your intimate Daddy. Now you have received the Spirit of adoption, *"producing sonship"* in *"the bliss of which"* you can now cry, *"Abba, (Father)! Father!"* (Romans 8:15, AMP).

Lou Engle says this cry to "Abba" is "the deepest primordial cry of the human heart."[9] And God's Word agrees: *"Because you [really] are [His] sons, God has sent the [Holy] Spirit of His Son into our hearts, crying, Abba (Father)! Father!"* (Galatians 4:6, AMP).

Now, as God looks down and sees your generation exploding in abandoned worship, His heart can no longer hold back the flood. It is just like the Bible says, *"He will come like a pent-up flood that the breath of the LORD drives along"* (Isaiah 59:19).

Finally, He can bear it no longer. The river of revival is ready to burst its bounds. Now, suddenly, it erupts from His pent-up heart. It roars from within Him, tumbling down from the throne, coursing over Heaven, rushing down upon planet Earth.

It streams over mountains and gushes into plains, searching out riverbeds—the low places of this earth. It splashes over rocks and soaks into crevices—the dugout places in human souls. At last, the revival finds a dwelling place—the cracked and broken hearts of a fatherless generation.

No wonder Satan so fears you! No wonder he has wiped out more than forty million through abortion! He saw the swelling throng, the revival generation, targeted by Abba Father before the foundation of the world.

This is the same river John the apostle saw as He looked into Heaven and saw a river, *"flowing out from the throne of God and of the Lamb."* It's *"the river whose waters give life"* (Revelation 22:1, AMP). So let that river of life flow down on you, and see your dying generation spring up with resurrection life from God.

Splashing in the River

One night the Holy Spirit descended with such power on some college men and women at our camp that I stood back and watched in absolute awe. It was spring break, and we had invited students from around the nation to come stay at our camp and attend the revival.

Every day, revival students who lived here at the camp prayed over them, and I watched the presence of God come plunging down upon them. Young adults, over-come with God's presence, fell to the floor trembling. I listened as they sang love songs to Jesus and prayed over one another, prophesying and encouraging each other in the Lord. Some laughed hilariously in the Spirit.

As they frolicked in the river, I realized that although many would criticize this, God Himself must be look-ing down with delight. I thought of the delight I used to feel when I watched my adorable twin babies splash-ing in the bath water. Barely able to sit up, they giggled and laughed, splashing one another and sloshing around in the water, even trying to swim.

I tried to imagine what God was feeling right then, as He looked down on His kids—giggling, laughing, splash-ing, washing, weeping, and swimming in His river. Although critics may stand along the banks to condemn their behavior, I was sure that God must be looking down with pleasure on His kids splashing in the river, *"whose streams make glad the city of God"* (Psalm 46:4).

Our Father knows the intense pain Jesus experienced as He birthed these in blood on the cross, and now He revives them in the river that pours from His heart. Just like a mom watching her babies splashing in the tub, I believe His heart bursts with delight as He watches them laughing and falling, weeping, leaping, and rejoicing in Him.

Now, at the end of the age, God has released a river of revival upon a whole generation, soaking the wounds of the fatherless. Won't you come to His river? Like a little child, toeing the edge of a pool in the summertime, go ahead and plunge in. Submerge yourself in the cooling streams and splash to your heart's content.

Dip your heart in the living, loving waters that pour from the heart of God. This river streams from Him and through Him and back again to Him. It's here for you to enjoy—a river rolling down from the heart of the Lamb.

Endnotes:

1. John Kilpatrick, *Feast of Fire* (Pensacola: John Kilpatrick, 1995), pp. 3-4.
2. In Kilpatrick's own words: "Suddenly, I felt a wind blow through my legs, just like in the second chapter of the book of Acts. A strong breeze went through my legs and suddenly both my ankles flipped over so that I could hardly stand. I thought, 'That's weird!' 'O God,' I prayed, 'What in the world is happening?' I stood on the sides of my ankles, unable to get my footing. I literally could not straighten up my feet.
   After receiving help from one of the men, Kilpatrick stepped to the microphone and shouted, "Folks, this is it. The Lord is here. Get in, get in!" He said, "I realized God had come and He had answered our prayers for revival." Then Steve Hill, the visiting evangelist whom God used to ignite the revival, walked by and waved his hand in the pastor's direction. "More, Lord," Steve said, and Pastor Kilpatrick hit the marble floor again, where he lay for almost four hours (Kilpatrick, *Feast of Fire*, pp. 76-77.
3. Interestingly, in 1991, four years before the outbreak in Pensacola, David Yonggi Cho, pastor of the world's largest church, was praying for revival in America. Burdened over the spiritual decline in this country, Cho said, "As I prayed, I felt the Lord prompt me to get a map of America, and to point my finger on the map. I found myself pointing to the city of Pensacola in the Florida panhandle." He sensed the Lord say to him, "I am going to send revival to the seaside city of Pensacola, and it will spread like a fire until all of America has been consumed by it." (David Yonggi Cho, "Foreword," in *Feast of Fire*, p. vii).
4. God's promise to be a Father to the fatherless is found in many biblical passages. See, for instance, Psalms 10:14 and 18, 68:5, 82:3, 146:9, Hosea 14:3, and James 1:27.
5. Charles G. Finney, *Revival Lectures* (Old Tappan, NJ: Fleming H. Revell Company, n.d.), p. 7.
6. Lou Engle, *Fast Forward: A Call to the Millennial Prayer Revolution* (Pasadena, CA: cu@dc, 1999), p. 13.
7. Richard Crisco, *It's Time: Passing Revival to the Next Generation* (Shippensburg, PA: Revival Press, 1997), p. x.
8. A physician's view of Jesus' heart failure: "Apparently, to make doubly sure of death, the legionnaire drove his lance between the ribs, upward through the pericardium and into the heart. John 19:34 states, '*And immediately there came out blood and water.*' Thus there was an escape of watery fluid from the sac surrounding the heart and the blood of the interior of the heart. This is rather conclusive postmortem evidence that Jesus died, not the usual crucifixion death by suffocation, but of heart failure due to shock and constriction of the

heart by fluid in the pericardium." (Dr. C. Truman Davis, "A Physician Analyzes the Crucifixion," www.forefunner.com/mandate/x0040_A _Physician_ Analyzes.html).

Jonathan Edwards, referring to the heart of Christ breaking open, said, "Revenging justice then spent all its force upon him, on account of our guilt; which made him sweat blood, and cry out upon the cross, and probably rent his vitals—broke his heart, the fountain of blood, or some other blood vessels—and by the violent fermentation turned his blood to water. For the blood and water that issued out of his side, when pierced by the spear, seems to have been extravasated blood; and so there might be a kind of literal fulfillment of Psalm 22:14, *'I am poured out like water, and all my bones are out of joint; my heart is like wax, it is melted in the midst of my bowels.'*" Jonathan Edwards, "The Excellency of Christ," *The Works of Jonathan Edwards,* Vol. I (Edinburgh: Banner of Truth Trust, 1995), p. 684.

"In his crucifixion, Christ did not sweat blood, as he had done before; not because his agony was not now so great, but his blood had vented another way. But although he did not sweat blood, yet such was the sufferings of his soul, that probably it rent his vitals; when his side was pierced, there came forth blood and water." Jonathan Edwards, "The History of the Work of Redemption," *Works,* Vol. I, p. 579.

9. Lou Engle, in a message given in May 1996, at Harvest Rock Church in Pasadena, CA.

Desperate Hunger

Desperate for Jesus

Chapter 3

Desperate Hunger

Shhh! ... Listen! ... Listen closely. Can you hear it? You can if you listen with your heart. Can you feel it? Feel the thunder as it fills the air—rising, rushing, gushing, pouring, roaring. Sense the raw power barreling down from the Father's throne. Look more closely ... It pours from the wounds of the Son, and it spills down upon a fatherless generation.

Do you know why He chose you? I believe it is because He sees within you an insatiable hunger. Because you are a forsaken generation, many of you have an aching void inside.

Every person has a vacuum in his or her soul, and it's a vacuum for God, but yours goes deeper because of your feelings of abandonment. The void inside you is one that only God Himself can fill. It's a gnawing hunger for a true Father.

Who's Hungry?

I believe that God looks down from Heaven, searching for those who are hungry for His presence. As Tommy Tenney says, "He only cares about your answer to one question: Do you want Me?"[1]

If your answer is a thundering YES, the Lord races to the roar of your cry for more of Him. Tenney explains, "God is just waiting to be caught by someone whose hunger exceeds his grasp."[2]

And once you've tasted His presence, nothing else can satisfy. It's like the insatiable appetite of a newborn babe. The first time warm milk touches an infant's lips, the baby doesn't know what to do, but hunger drives her. She fumbles with the nipple, and for the first time, she sucks. In flows the warm, sweet milk.

The milk slips down and soaks into the raw place in her stomach, and something within her responds, *Ahhhh! ... This is it! This satisfies my hunger*.

It's the same with you. Something inside you hungers—ravenously. You don't know what will satisfy your hunger until it has actually touched your lips. But then, when a taste of the Lord's warm, sweet wine has touched your mouth, something within you gulps. The living presence of God slips in and touches the raw place in the belly of your soul, and you, too, say, *"Ahhh! ... This is it! This satisfies my hunger like nothing I've ever experienced in my whole life!"*

Now you're ravenous for more. Like a baby, not knowing how to drink but sucking fiercely, you haven't known how to worship or how to pray. But suddenly you are just doing it. A roaring hunger drives you, and now you're drinking furiously. And, even as a baby can never go back to receiving nourishment through an umbilical cord, you realize that you too can never go back.

You're forever ruined by the river. Nothing else satisfies but the pure, warm presence of God. And it comes, bubbling with life, tumbling down on your generation.

Most of us in the older generations are so acclimated to the stale air of religion we don't realize that God wants to breathe the fresh air of His presence into our lungs. I believe you yearn to be flooded with the rarefied air of revival. You crave for God to be the very air you breathe.

You see, God waits until we are desperate for His presence. He delays until He sees us so hungry for Him that our insides ache to be filled with more. He pauses to hear us crying for more as *"[roaring] deep cries to [roaring] deep"* (Psalm 42:7, AMP).

Some of you might say, "I'm too reserved. I don't want to lose my dignity." But Jesus said you must become like little children. You must be willing to strip off your robes of dignity, like David did (see 2 Samuel 6:14 and 21), and abandon yourself to God.

That's why I want to encourage you to run to the nearest revival, strip off your outer clothes of religion, and dive unprotected into the waters. Take a refreshing swim, and you'll be ruined for routine church services. Even many Charismatic or Pentecostal services, without the spirit of revival, won't be enough to slake your thirst.

Once you've breathed the purified air of revival, the stuffy atmosphere of dead churches will no longer satisfy your cravings. Like David's, your heart will languish for God's presence *"as the hart pants and longs for the water brooks"* (Psalm 42:1, AMP).

Once you drink of the sweet wine of Heaven, although it will satisfy, you'll thirst for more and more. As A.W. Tozier said, "To have found God and still to pursue Him is the soul's paradox of love."[3] Quoting St. Bernard, Tozier wrote:

> We taste Thee, O Thou Living Bread,
> And long to feast upon Thee still:
> We drink of Thee, the Fountainhead,
> And thirst our souls from Thee to fill.[4]

Feel the Roar

I tell you, I'm broken by what I see in the young men and women here in Pensacola. I have never seen or felt such growling hunger for God. I believe the Lord is stirring this hunger in all who will receive it, especially among those of your generation.

Have you heard this roar? Have you felt it? It's like a rising groundswell, spreading through your whole generation and bursting out in explosions of passionate worship and prayer.

The first time I heard the roar was in the middle of the night. It was 2:45 A.M., and I was awakened to a strange sound. Students from the ministry school were living at my camp, and that particular night they were praying. I couldn't believe my ears. Passion is an understatement. It was a crying, groaning, sobbing, bellowing roar like I had never heard in my life. I wanted to get up and see if the young men were all right, but I was afraid to tread into such holiness.

The next morning the students released prophetic words to me that changed my life. It was as though a thin veneer had been covering my soul, and now it had been stripped away. Then I began to hear the roar more clearly for myself.

A few days later, I joined the evangelism team from Brownsville Revival School of Ministry. I walked in a few minutes late, and what I saw staggered me. I saw hundreds of students, most under twenty-five, pounding Heaven. They walked through the room, shouting, crying, roaring to God in prayer.

None of the professors from the school were there, so these students weren't trying to impress anyone. All over the room young men and women were pleading with tears, in prayer for souls. After two hours, we all jumped into cars and headed toward the inner city and the beach, to lead the lost to Jesus.

I had considered myself to be a soulwinner, and had led many people to the Lord, but something about this experience was different. I joined Freddie, an Hispanic-American from Chicago, and we teamed up to win souls on the beach. Freddie had been on drugs and had come out of poverty. He knew the pain of the father-less generation. I listened as he preached, quoting scripture after scripture. It wasn't robotic or mechanical; it was life-giving and relational. I watched drunken young men and women swagger up and listen in rapt attention.

Then I began to realize one of the reasons this revival reaches so many young men and women. These guys are going after souls with burning passion. The roar of hunger and the blaze of revival impels and propels them into the hard places. It drives them into the highways and byways. It carries them to the poor, and especially to the lost and even out to other nations.

The sound of this passion and desperate hunger in your generation is bursting forth across America. I saw it explode in youth groups who came to our Camp America Ablaze. After the first night, kids who had never done this before were weeping, moaning, and bellowing out to God in prayer. When one of their lost young men gave in to God's drawing and got saved, they screamed and roared in explosions of praise.

This reminds me of Noah's flood, when the windows of Heaven opened and poured down a deluge from above. But even more, the fountains of the great deep gushed forth from the ground (see Genesis 7:11). When the two forces came together, the whole earth was flooded with water.

Tommy Tenney explains, "When brokenness appears in our lives, openness appears in the heavens."[5] This is why I believe you are able to "rip open the veil" into God's manifest presence with your prayers. You are a broken generation. Your emptiness creates volumes for Him to fill. As Tenney says, "The volume of your emptiness determines the amount of your filling."[6]

That's why the cry of a fatherless generation has pierced the heart of God and released a deluge of powerful revival. Now, the fountains of the great deep within each young man and woman are breaking up and bursting forth. I believe this bursting river will continue to flow until the whole earth is filled with the glory of the Lord, as the waters cover the seas (see Habakkuk 2:14).

Don't Let Your Hunger Dissipate

What will you do, however, when friends mock you or older people try to dampen this holy roar by accusing you of being fanatical or superspiritual or downright weird? Will you "cave"? Please don't let your passion dim or your hunger diminish. It happened to me, so I speak from experience.

I want to be vulnerable with you now, so you can learn from my mistake. Years ago (in the early 1980s) I was so hungry for God's presence. I taught on the glory of God and His manifest presence, and the Lord released an anointing such as I had never experienced before.

But in those days, very few people taught on the glory, and some leaders came to me to correct me. They told me that what I thought was God's presence wasn't really Him. They urged me to teach on God's love, not His glory, which, they said, was "spooky." I apologized to them and repented before God, asking Him to take away this "presence"—whatever it was.

But when I found the river of revival at Harvest Rock Church in Pasadena in 1995, I realized the mistake I had made. I saw then that I had wounded the Holy Spirit by rejecting His glory. This broke my heart, and I was compelled to repent of having repented previously.

Though God has now restored the glory of His presence to my life, I lost many years by allowing cold water to splash on my fire. I was young then, and easily crushed, and I unintentionally grieved the Holy Spirit by listening to others.

I let the fear of what they thought drown out my fear of what God thought, and, consequently, the next fourteen years were difficult ones for me. Once I found revival and began to soak my weary heart in its shining streams, God began restoring my passion for His manifest presence, for His glory.

The Lord showed me that this is all He really looks for in us. It's our hunger for His presence that draws Him. That gentle ache for God's presence that burns so deep in one's soul causes Him to draw near. As Tenney says, God is "drawn to the empty capacity of our growling spiritual stomachs."[7]

Tenney's books, *The God Chasers* and *The God Catchers*, did even more to restore my waning hunger. Then, when he started preaching once a month at Brownsville, fresh hunger came to all of us.[8] The first time I heard him in the spring of 2001, his message was simple, but our hearts were utterly melted by what he said. That gentle ache for more of God stirred in us. People began to weep and wail. I bent over, sobbing, repenting to the Lord for having allowed people to subdue my hunger.

When I rose from my face, after weeping in godly sorrow, I was consumed once again with a burning hunger for God. I could feel again that sweet ache for His presence. I can't even talk about it now without crying, but I really feel that some of you have experienced the same wounding. Someone mocked your passion or scoffed at your voracious hunger, and maybe it caused you to pull back and become lukewarm, and thus more acceptable to others. This is nothing less than allowing the fear of man to outweigh the holy fear of God. Tommy Tenney asks, "How long has it been since you've been so hungry for God that it consumed you to the point you couldn't care less what people thought of you?"[9]

If this is you, if you have let the fear of what others think keep you from abandoned worship, won't you tell Him how sorry you are? Repent to Him for having grieved His Holy Spirit. Strip off this fear of what others think, and run to the river of God. And don't let anything or anyone ever again mar or dissipate your passionate search for more of God.

A true story is told of a little boy who came early every day to light the potbellied coal stove for his schoolhouse. One morning the teacher arrived to find the school engulfed in flames, and the boy was still inside. They were able to drag him out, but the lower half of his body was horribly burned.

To the physician's amazement, the boy survived, but because the fire had destroyed so much flesh on the lower part of his body, he would be hopelessly crippled the rest of his life. The little boy, however, refused this diagnosis. He fixed his eyes on the goal. He *would* walk again.

Every day he wheeled himself out to the yard, threw himself from his wheelchair, pulled himself across the grass, and took hold of the white picket fence. Stake by stake, he would drag himself along the fence until a smooth path was worn around the yard by his exercises.

Finally, because of his resolute determination, he was able to stand alone and then to walk, though haltingly.

He soon began to walk to school, and then to run. For the sheer joy of running, he started racing every day to school. In college, he tried out for the track team and made it.

Years later, a crowd at Madison Square Garden leapt to their feet, cheering and applauding as Glenn Cunningham—the boy with the burned and crippled legs—ran the world's fastest mile.[10]

How did he do it? He fixed his eyes on a goal and never gave up. That's what you can do, too, as you run after God with all your heart and soul and strength.

Run to the River

So listen again ... Can you hear it? Can you feel it burning in your belly? Can you sense the heat on your face and the tingle in your hands? God is releasing a river upon you.

The cry of a fatherless generation has pierced the heart of God and released the deluges of Heaven. Let the river come. Let it spill and fill and cleanse the wounds in your soul.

Let it infuse you so fully that you will feel the pent-up flood carrying you along on its currents. Again, it is just like the Bible promises, *"He will come like a pent-up flood that the breath of the LORD drives along"* (Isaiah 59:19).

Like the pounding waters of a massive waterfall, come close to the raw power of the falls and soak in the goodness of God.

Soak it into your soul. But this time come even closer. Be like those who stand under the ledge of the falls, so close they can almost reach out and touch the gushing currents. Here the sound is deafening. The uproar is overwhelming. It is the power of God, exploding over the cliffs and surging in billows of glory.

Let that power come on you. Let the sound of revival fill you. Let the river Jesus died to pour out upon this world surge down upon you. Let it come. Drink and drink and drink some more. Drink with all your heart, and let it fill and fill you until you are satisfied.

Once you do this, you'll never be the same. Everything within you will cry for this river. Your thirst will burn. It will be insatiable, for the more you drink, the thirstier you'll become. The Holy Spirit Himself will fill you with a desperate hunger for God.

Endnotes:

1. Tommy Tenney, *The God Chasers* (Shippensburg, PA: Destiny Image, 1998), p. 11.
2. Tommy Tenney, *The God Chasers*, p. i.
3. A.W. Tozier, *The Pursuit of God* (Camp Hill, PA: Christian Publications, Inc., 1982), p. 15.
4. A.W. Tozier, *The Pursuit of God*, p. 15.
5. Tommy Tenney, *The God Catchers* (Nashville: Thomas Nelson Publishers, 2000), p. 25.
6. Tommy Tenney, *The God Catchers*, p. 107.
7. Tommy Tenney, *The God Catchers*, p. 112.
8. Tommy Tenney, *The God Catchers*, p. 12.
9. Tommy Tenney, *The God Chasers*, p. 13.
10. Jack Canfield and Mark Victor Hansen, "The Power of Determination" (Deerfield Beach, FL: Health Communications, Chicken Soup for the Soul, Inc., 1993), pp. 259-260.

Camp America Ablaze Photo

Lost in Worship

A
Postmodern
Pentecost

Staggering Through a Prayer Tunnel

Chapter 4

A Postmodern Pentecost

"Watch!" the Holy Spirit whispered to me one day in a chapel service at Brownsville Revival School of Ministry. "This is how I will spread revival throughout America and the world!" Then I sat back and watched a thousand students walk through revival fire.

Several hundred graduating students had formed two rows, creating a prayer tunnel. As students and faculty alike walked through the two rows, the presence and power of Jesus mounted. Soon it exploded through the entire sanctuary.

As students and professors stumbled through the line, the hands of the prayer team barely touched them. It was hardly necessary. God was there. In the widest stretch of my imagination, I could not have conceived that the original Pentecost had been any more powerful than what I saw and felt that day. This was indeed a postmodern Pentecost, as young men and women prayed for one another with roaring hearts.

Most amazing to me was that God wasn't using famous evangelists and pastors to spread His power.

Nameless, faceless students exploded with His presence and imparted the fire of revival to one another.

As I sat in awe, watching the outbreak of revival among the young, I knew this was the answer God has reserved to meet the mountainous obstacles of our day. One of those mountains is the massive upheaval brought on by what is termed the Postmodern Age.

Postmodern Times

Please don't "zone out" on me as I briefly touch on a rather heavy subject. The Postmodern Age is the name historians have given to an epoch of human history, just as the Middle Ages, the Age of Enlightenment, and the Modern Age were periods of time, each lasting hundreds of years. According to historians, we have now entered the Postmodern Age. Though I certainly don't suggest that you should agree with the hazy philosophy of this postmodern era, you do need to realize that it has influenced the thinking of your generation, and you need to gain an understanding of it so that you can face the monumental challenge it presents.

If you were born between 1965 and 1983, you are part of the first postmodern generation. All those who have birth dates following 1965 are considered postmodernists, which means that their thinking has been shaped by a philosophical shift.

Tim Celek and Dieter Zander, youth pastors at Bill Hybels' church in the suburbs of Chicago, have said, "Postmodernity (another name for a postmodern era), in our opinion, is the single most powerful force in shaping the mindset, attitudes, and values of the buster generation."[1]

So many Christian ministers, authors, and even secular conservatives, such as Allan Bloom in his bestselling *The Closing of the American Mind*, don't seem to understand the postmodern influence. They express bewilderment over the relative thinking of your generation. That's because they are thinking with a modern mindset, rather than a postmodern understanding.

James Emery White said, "The postmodern generation may well be the most difficult generation in the history of Western civilization to reach with the Gospel." He concluded, "Never has such a challenge been before us; never has the opportunity for making a difference been so great."[2] However, after writing my Ph.D. dissertation entitled "Revival Among America's First Postmodern Generation," I knew without a doubt that revival is God's answer for meeting the challenges of postmodernity.

Now hang with me just a little longer and let me show you why, for this has profound ramifications for the grand sweep of revival in America through your generation.

Modern and Postmodern Times

When the Enlightenment ushered in the modern era, sometimes called modernity, revelation from God became replaced by reason, logic, and rationality.[3] Theism, or belief in God, was replaced by humanism, a belief in man. Faith in the Bible was replaced by science. The modern era held idealistic hopes of a utopian society brought about by evolution, scientific progress, and human ingenuity.

The tide of modernity, however, with its idealism, began to recede with the onslaught of two world wars. The shock of learning that six million Jews had been annihilated in death camps caused the idea of a perfect world through human progress to begin to die.

Then, in the late 1960s, the heart of America broke. With the assassinations of John and Bobby Kennedy and Martin Luther King, Jr., hope for the future shattered. Psychedelic drugs, sexual liberty, and anger over a meaningless war in Vietnam slithered into the crack in the soul of America.

All this time, God reached out and beckoned to the young generation, your parents. He poured out His Spirit in the Charismatic Movement among young adults. He breathed on the hippies, causing the Jesus Movement to arise among the young, but still, many resisted His mercy.

By 1989, the tide of modernity, with its vision for a perfect world through human progress, was forever swept out to sea, and the tidal wave of postmodernity, with its skepticism, relative thinking, and meaninglessness, had broken over the shores of time. Some have been slow to grasp these changes, but today a new way of thinking has prevailed in the Western world. In the late 1980s a new era of relativity had dawned. The turn was, as Russia's Aleksandr Solzhenitsyn said, "as dramatic as the turn from the Middle Ages to the Renaissance."[4]

Now here's what's important to get for our purposes

in revival: In a postmodern era, *community* replaces individualism, *irrationality* replaces reason, *pessimism* replaces optimism and idealism, *tolerance of all ideas* replaces absolute truths, *subjectivism* replaces objectivism, *feelings* and *emotions* replace logic and intellectualism, and *relativity* replaces science.

Do you see now why the young generation views life so differently than their parents do? It's bigger than the difference between the baby boomers and the so-called baby busters. It's a whole new philosophical paradigm shift.

To modernists—which would be your parents, those of my generation—truth is rational, understood through intellect, logic, and dogmatic absolutes; to postmodernists—your generation—truth is not rational, but is reached through feelings, emotion, and experience. To a modernist, truth is absolute, it is objective, and it does not contradict itself; to a postmodernist, truth is subjective, and several contradicting "truths" can stand together.

To the modernist mind, human idealism and progress are our hope; to a postmodernist, there is no hope because there is no absolute truth. Modernists esteem rugged individualism; postmodernists value community and relationships. To a modernist, time is money; to a postmodernist, time is meaningful only when spent in relationships with people. While modernists tolerate hypocrisy, postmodernists must have authenticity and pure reality.

But do you see what this means to us? Again, I'm not suggesting that we fall into the foggy thinking of a postmodern philosophy, simply that we understand it. What I am suggesting is that we find a higher way, and

I'm absolutely convinced that revival is that higher way.[5] Revival is God's divine answer to the postmodern challenge.

God's Answer

Now, as I sat in chapel and watched a thousand young men and women exploding with joy, I knew this was God's answer for postmodernity. Students leapt and danced like David. They clapped and shouted and cried. Heika, a German singer, who had given up a soaring career in Europe, sang the fire down. As she sang and the students prayed, the power of God burned so hotly down upon them that many had to be carried, literally, back to their seats.

I thought to myself, *This is what young postmodern men and women are looking for. They have little interest in dogma and logical apologetics. They hunger for a divine encounter with God. They burn for an experience with Christ, not an intellectual understanding. They yearn for a postmodern Pentecost.*

I was thoroughly caught up in the awe and wonder of the raw power of God flowing through students to other students, and I realized that this generation refuses hypocrisy, hype, and dead religion. What they are experiencing right now is totally real. This is the genuine presence of God, and it fills their deepest longings.[6]

Though scholars may shudder and critics may scoff, sound doctrine and apologetics will not reach your generation. You must first *experience* the One who suffered your pain and shame and knows the feeling of a tear slipping down the skin of His cheek.

That's why revival is God's answer to the postmodern challenge. Never in American history has a single generation been so rejected, abused, and misunderstood. But when you experience the presence of God sweeping down upon you until your heart shakes, you know He is alive.

Revival Is the Answer

Staleness often filled the intellectual air of modernity, and now death and hopelessness fill the skeptical air of postmodernity. But since revival is "breathing in the breath of God," this is just what we need. Revival refreshes every cell and corpuscle of the body, filling the bloodstream with the very life of God.

Revival meets the postmodern need for feelings and emotions, but it also goes deeper. It kindles and rekindles faith. It inflames pure love. It stirs emotions and brings down the tangible reality of the manifest presence of God.

Revival consumes the irrationality and skepticism of postmodernity. It burns through the fog of relative values by showing how God feels about His values. Revival displays His holiness and creates within the hungry soul a desire for Christ-like character.

Revival fills the hopelessness of a postmodern generation with hope and purpose and passion. It also causes God's Word to suddenly blaze with truth.

Yes, revival meets the postmodern need for an experience, but it is much more. This generation wants an encounter with God that "goes deeper than the cerebral cortex," wrote Chaplain Ben Patterson after the outbreak of confessions at Hope College in 1995. "They don't want a faith that goes against reason, but they do want a faith that goes further. They understand with Pascal that 'the heart has reasons which reason does not know.' "[7]

Without absolutes, your generation finds it difficult to relate to the concept of sin ... that is, until you come into an experience with the holiness of God. With the burning revelation of His love pouring down upon you in revival, you are the first to fall on your faces in repentance.

By postmodern standards, the absolute truth of the Gospel and the high calling to holiness should fly right over the heads of a postmodern generation. But when seeds of truth are carried on flames of revival, they burn straight into the hearts of young postmodernists.

Peek inside the Brownsville Revival on a Friday night and see young men and women race to the altar and fall on their knees in repentance. As the evangelist unsheathes the sword of the Spirit and drives it straight into the heart of sin, young people bolt toward the altar and throw themselves to their knees, sobbing. They cry out desperately for forgiveness, weeping in repentance until all their sins are washed away in the red sea of the Savior's blood.

When Steve Hill was still at Brownsville, he preached an in-your-face Gospel to postmodern youth and young adults, and they loved it. Pastor Richard Crisco explained that the reason people received from Steve Hill, although he confronted them with their sin, was because he did it "with tears streaming down his face."[8] Crisco continued:

> This generation wants Steve Hill to get in their face. They want him to point his finger and say, "Young man, stop masturbating. Young lady, stop jumping into bed." They want somebody to tell them not to do those things.[9]

Except on special occasions, Steve Hill no longer preaches at Brownsville, for God has released him to the nations. But under John Kilpatrick's leadership, God's presence remains powerful in the church. The revival continues on Thursday and Friday nights, and the spirit of revival is bursting from the school. As a teacher at Brownsville Revival School of Ministry, I have reason to know that the Holy Spirit is given first priority in classes. If He sweeps in, teachers move out of the way and let Him take full control.

Your generation rejects the hypocrisy, the dry orthodoxy, the religious hype and ritual of many baby-boomer churches today.[10] But I have listened to the stories of young men and women turning from pornography, drugs, and alcoholism. I have heard confessions of homosexuality, of promiscuity, and of thoughts of suicide, and I know how real they are.

Nothing rings with such bare-bones reality as the tangible presence of God in revival. Spiritual movements come and go, but revival comes from Heaven. Its impact is eternal. Revival towers far above the earthly realm of postmodernity, for revival comes from the Lamb.

Yes, a postmodern era has swept over the globe, but spanning far above the circle of time, rising above the confusion, and spiraling upward between earth and Heaven, is the cross of Jesus Christ. Pull back the veil and look upon the throne, and there you will see the One who once bled upon a cross, but who still bleeds upon His throne.

There He stands, a Lamb, looking as though He's been slain. And pouring from the Lamb comes a river of revival. That's why revival far transcends a postmodern era. It surpasses every era. It spills from the heart of a wounded Lamb and brings life everywhere it flows.

Revival brings a revelation of Christ to your souls, and this revelation transcends the intellectual doctrine and objectivity of a modern era. It rises above the subjectivity and irrationality of a postmodern era, for truth is ultimately found, not in a concept, but in a Person. Think for a moment how Jesus relates to your generation.

Jesus for a Postmodern Generation

Jesus only lived to be thirty-three, which today would still be the age of the postmodern generation. And like today's postmodernists, He walked into a world torn apart by violence, injustice, and bloodshed.

Like postmodern youth today, He was genuinely authentic and down-to-earth. He never wanted a lofty title, though He was God of the universe. He simply wanted to be called by a humble human name, Jesus.

Relationships meant everything to Jesus. He never placed money, power, or position over people, as modernistic baby boomers have often done. Jesus wasn't career driven; He was love-driven. Like yours, His heart thundered with love for hurting, sick, grieving underdogs of humanity.

Jesus couldn't tolerate the hypocrisy and sham of some of the religious leaders of His day. He never tried to reach people through intellect or logic, but rather through feelings, through emotion, through the human heart. He opened up the fathomless mysteries of God, but He didn't do it with highbrow intellectualism. He did it by asking questions, telling stories, and showing His love through miracles and healings.

Though He was God, He experienced the reality of human pain and suffering. He knew the feeling of wet tears sliding down His face and soaking into His beard. In fact, so that He could know the feeling of teardrops swelling in His eyes and running down His cheeks, He laid aside His garments of glory and clothed himself in human skin.

Only then could Jesus experience the ache of rejection, the pain of abuse and molestation, the pounding throb of a broken heart, the wetness of a human tear, the terror of one's very own warm human blood dripping from a wound. That's why, when He hung suspended between Heaven and earth on two slabs of timber, tears splashing and human spittle splotching His cheeks, He swept the crowd with His eyes. I believe He saw more than a little crowd of followers huddled around the cross.

I believe that in that moment Jesus looked ahead with divine foresight and saw a young generation crossing the postmodern divide, carrying hearts that ached for a father. He saw your pain, your shattered dreams, your broken homes, your wounded hearts. He heard the silent cry, bellowing from the soul of your generation. It was a cry for a father, a cry for a family ... most of all, a cry for God. If the cry could be formed into words, it was "My God, why have even You forsaken me?"

Jesus cried your cry from the cross, and now He runs to the sound of your cry. Just like the father of the prodigal son, He races over the hillside, throws His arms around you, and kisses away your pain.

Now, He wants you to come to the banquet, where He will clothe you with Himself. Now, you can drink from the new wine of revival and feed on the fatness of His presence. Now, He is calling you to rise up and go out, lifting high the cross of the Lamb in the midst of the dark and uncharted waters of postmodernity.

This is why we must understand the times, for revival is God's answer for the postmodern challenge.

Think of it: At this watershed of human history, God has chosen *you*. You are America's first postmodern generation, but you are so much more.

You are the revival generation. God has chosen you to spread the rivers of revival over the land in a massive postmodern Pentecost!

Endnotes:

1. Tim Celek and Dieter Zander, *Inside the Soul of a New Generation* (Grand Rapids, MI: Zondervan Publishing House, 1996), p. 51.
2. James Emery White, "Evangelism in a Postmodern World," in *The Challenge of Postmodernism: An Evangelical Engagement,* David S. Dockery, ed., pp. 359-373 (Grand Rapids, MI: Baker Book House, 1995), p. 37.
3. Thomas C. Oden defined the modern era as "the period, the ideology, and the malaise of time from 1789 to 1989, from the Bastille to the Berlin Wall (Oden, "The Death of Modernity and Postmodern Spirituality," in *The Challenge of Postmodernism,* David S. Dockery, ed., pp. 19-33 [Grand Rapids, MI: Baker Book House, 1995], p. 20.
4. Aleksandr Solzhenitsyn, while speaking to a Harvard graduating class called for spiritual vision as we enter the unknown territory of postmodernity:
   If the world has not approached its end, it has reached a major watershed in history, equal in importance to the turn from the Middle Ages to the Renaissance. It will demand from us a spiritual upsurge; we shall have to rise to a new height of vision, to a new level of life, where our physical nature will not be cursed, as in the Middle Ages, but even more importantly, our spiritual being will not be trampled upon as in the Modern era (Aleksandr I. Solzhenitsyn, "A World Split Apart," a speech given at Harvard University, 1978, p. 9. See www/hunews.Harvard.edu/hno.subpages/speeches/solzhenitsyn.html.
5. Charles Van Engen, professor of Mission Theology at Fuller Theological Seminary and my mentor at Fuller, said, "It is imperative that evangelicals take seriously the critique of modernity—but it is equally imperative that we offer our postmodern world a more excellent way" (Van Engen, *Mission on the Way: Issues in Mission Theology* [Grand Rapids, MI: Baker Book House, 1996], p. 221).
6. The power of God in revival meets the postmodern need for fellowship in community and relationships. But the presence of God in revival melts through the skepticism of postmodernity and provides true hope. It transcends the reason and rationality of modernity, but it reaches higher than postmodern relativism. Furthermore, revival is the flame that sears through the intellectualism of modernity and torches the irrational haze of postmodernity. It melts through the dogma and cool logic of modernity and ignites the feelings of the soul. Most of all, revival fills the ache in the heart of a fatherless generation, bringing them into a face-to-face encounter with the fatherhood of God.
7. Ben Patterson, *Perspectives* 10(6), p.13.
8. Richard Crisco, *It's Time: Passing Revival to the Next Generation* (Shippensburg, PA: Revival Press, 1997), p. 54.
9. Richard Crisco, *It's Time*, p. 54.
10. Kevin Ford said that if you ask a non-Christian in your generation "what it means to be a Christian," he will probably answer, "a hypocrite," or "someone who's intolerant," or "someone from the religious right." He said, "Don't expect to hear, 'someone who authentically loves people and actively lives out a relationship with Jesus Christ.' " He continued, "One cultural barrier that divides pre-Christian Xers from the story of Jesus Christ is the 'bad Christian' stereotype—a stereotype that is all too often true." Kevin Graham Ford, *Jesus for a New Generation: Putting the Gospel in the Language of Xers* (Downers Grove, IL: InterVarsity Press, 1995), p. 48.

Overwhelmed by the Presence of God

America
Ablaze

Imparting to Students

Chapter 5

America Ablaze

As young men and women staggered through the prayer line at the Brownsville Revival School of Ministry chapel service, I could visibly see the effects of the Holy Spirit upon them. Their faces burned and glowed, some quite red, from the heat of the flame of God's Spirit. Many trembled and shook. Tears washed almost every face. Most of all, the power and presence of God blazed and filled the large sanctuary.

Now I was beginning to understand what the Lord meant when He had said, "This is how I will spread revival to America and to all the world!"

Impartations of Revival

Some question the fact that revival can actually be imparted through people. I know it seems strange, but this is the way God often spreads revival. Just as the baptism in the Holy Spirit is often imparted through the laying on of other people's hands (see Acts 19:6), the spirit of revival also can be transferred through the laying on of hands.

77

When Peter Wagner and Ed Silvoso appeared on a TBN television program in 1996, they invited the listening audience to a "Light the Nation" conference to receive "impartations" of revival from the Argentine revivalists. I went to that conference, and I saw thousands receiving impartations of revival fire.

So powerful were the manifestations, after the revivalists laid hands on us, that people had to be carried out and laid in the hallway of the Dallas Convention Center. Many trembled and shook and burned under the overwhelming power of God's presence. They had received an impartation of revival from the Argentines—just as Peter Wagner had promised.

I know that some might question these manifestations, but I experienced true fruit resulting from this power. While still under that wonderful anointing, I walked outside and prayed with five Muslim taxi drivers. When a policeman tried to wave the taxis away, I walked over to the policeman and asked if he would like to receive Jesus Christ as his Savior, too.

To my astonishment, he indicated that he would. So, right there in the middle of the street in front of the Dallas Convention Center, I prayed with him to receive Christ. I could feel the power of God flowing through me like an irresistible force, as it flowed out to the policeman and to the Muslim taxi drivers. This surely happened because of the impartation of revival burning upon me.

When a revival broke out at Southwestern Theological Seminary in 1995, Professor Roy Fish wrote a letter inviting people to come visit the outpouring. "When the fire is falling, get as near as you can to the flame!" he advised.[1]

Campus Crusade's Bill Bright explained, "Whenever any Christian whose heart is ignited with the fire of Heaven comes in touch with one whose heart is hungry for God but is presently living in spiritual defeat, another fire will be ignited."[2]

Now, as I sat in the chapel service at the ministry school and watched, these were not seasoned revivalists who were doing the ministering. These were young men and women in their early twenties, virtual nobodies in the eyes of the world. They were lightly touching other students and calling the fire of God down upon them. As students stumbled through the prayer line, the raw power of God exploded through the room.

Paul wrote to the Roman believers, *"I long to see you so that I may IMPART to you some spiritual gift to make you strong"* (Romans 1:11). I was visibly observing what Paul meant. These students were imparting a spiritual blessing on everyone they touched. I realized then that as this young generation of revolutionary firebrands went out, they would set *America Ablaze* with revival. They would lay hands on others, transferring the anointing of Jesus, which was flowing so powerfully through their own lives.

Some might suggest, "But won't the fire fizzle out and come to nothing?" It might. It depends on what one does with the fire. I know that after Heaven's flame touched me in the spring of 1995 at Ché Ahn's Harvest Rock Church, it eventually did dim. But the touch of fire had made me so hungry that I had to run after God until He touched me with more of His revival fire.

I kept chasing Him until finally a more permanent impartation rested upon me. If you are hungry—really hungry—you, too, will be willing to forsake all to go after this pearl of inestimable price.

It's like one young man who was baptized in water at Brownsville. Having turned from drugs to run after God, he cried, "Jesus, I'm so hungry it hurts! I'm so hungry it hurts! I'm so hungry it hurts!" When he was lowered into the water, the Holy Spirit met that hunger. So powerfully did the Lord come down upon Him that it took five men to carry him out of the baptismal pool.

Still, even the men carrying him out were knocked over by the power of God's Spirit pouring down on him. Seeing these powerful manifestations led me to start a revival camp for college students and other young people.

Our ministry team in the camp consists of revival students from the ministry school. I've watched them impart the flame of revival with shameless passion to those who come from around the nation. Then I've seen these students and other campers carry the spark back, igniting fires in their campuses, churches, and schools.

The fire of revival is indeed contagious. It burns and rolls like a literal fire. It spreads through impartation, just as it did in New Testament days. Those who were in the Upper Room on the Day of Pentecost carried the spirit of revival everywhere they went. They could now lay hands on others, and power poured out from them.

It did not happen, however, until they received that divine impartation from Heaven.

Paul, of course, wasn't in that upper room, so God gave him his own special encounter on the road to Damascus. This is why, if we want to be carriers of revival, we must have our own encounters with God. This may mean leaving your comfortable little corner to go where revival is happening. Again, as Dr. Fish said, "When the fire is falling, get as near as you can to the flame!"[3]

Faith or Feelings?

"But," you might ask, "how can we trust emotions? Aren't we supposed to walk by faith, not feeling?" My answer is simply this: With such brokenness and pain in your generation, you must have faith ablaze with emotion and feelings. You must have truth ignited with holy fire. Just like the two men who heard Jesus speak on the road to Emmaus (see Luke 24:32), you must have hearts that burn with flames of revival.

The concept of faith without feeling is a modernist concept. It is old-fashioned, outdated, and will not relate to your postmodern generation. To meet the postmodern challenge, you must have faith filled with feeling. Nothing else will speak to a wounded postmodern generation and to all generations to come.

Let the modernist critics complain, but your generation needs to have the void in your souls filled with the love of a supremely emotional God. A sixteen-year-old boy wrote me this simple note, which says it all:

At twelve, I lost my dad.
At fourteen, I lost my mom.
Then I found Jesus in the revival.[4]

So let the critics rail. I know you need a fire-filled faith that can heal your broken hearts.

Still, the modernists criticize revival among the young. When a revival of confession and repentance broke out at Hope College in 1995, a modern-day critic commented that revival is a passing fad like "streaking" or water frisbee.[5] I was appalled that anyone would dare compare the holy presence of God in revival to the crude obscenity of streaking. Your parents can tell you about the streaking that was practiced in the 1960s. It involved stripping naked and running down a street or across a college campus in the sight of some crowd of people. I blush to think what God must feel when revival is compared to nudity!

At the campus revival at Wheaton College in 1995, Professor Lyle Dorsett said that some were "outspokenly distressed over what was transpiring, calling it a display of emotionalism that was, at best, undignified."[6] I want to ask, however, where in the Bible are you taught to be dignified in your faith toward God? Can you show me a verse that calls you to be lukewarm? Jesus said He would spew us out of His mouth if we were lukewarm (see Revelation 3:15-16). He said He'd rather we be *cold or hot* for Him. The word He used that was translated *"hot"* is *zeo*, meaning "boiling." Jesus longs for you to be boiling hot in your faith. He wants you to have hearts that bubble and blaze with passion toward God.

That's why He urges us to love the Lord with all our heart and soul and mind and strength (see Mark 12:30). Paul exhorts us to *"never lag in zeal"* but always be *"aglow and burning with the Spirit"* (Romans 12:11, AMP). Again, the word is *zeo.* God wants us to be "boiling" in His Spirit.

In fact, our Lord Jesus prayed with *"loud cries and tears"* (Hebrews 5:7). He travailed with deep emotion over Jerusalem (see Luke 19:41). He wept at Lazarus' death. He often burst out with a *"loud voice"* when speaking to a crowd (for instance, see John 7:37). You see, our God is profoundly emotional. I'm not talking about emotionalism, which speaks of hype and manipulation. I mean genuine, gut-wrenching emotion, the kind Jesus demonstrated when He screamed out to God from the cross.

Revival or Rigor Mortis

Chaplain Ben Patterson of Hope College said, "The colossal failure of the church in the modern world suggests that what we need now is not so much restraint as arousal and awakening. That can be messy. But better the messiness of life than the orderliness of rigor mortis!"[7]

Without revival, your wounded generation is already showing signs of rigor mortis. Again, I must say, never in the history of America has a single generation so desperately needed the life-giving power of revival. When God looks down and breathes His Spirit upon you, a young generation will indeed rise from the dead.

Do you recall when Elijah stretched himself across a fatherless boy and breathed life into his nostrils (see 1 Kings 17)? Also, when a boy with a deadbeat dad, as Richard Crisco called him in a sermon, died in his mother's arms, she took the son to Elisha? The prophet stretched himself across the boy, *"mouth to mouth, eyes to eyes, hands to hands"* (2 Kings 4:34). Suddenly a boy with rigor mortis was raised to new life by the breath of God, through the prophet.

Furthermore, do you remember when Jesus raised a fatherless young man, the son of the widow of Nain, from the dead (see Luke 7:11)? I believe that God is saying something through these illustrations. He yearns to raise a fatherless generation from the dead. He will do it with the breath of God—revival—upon a lifeless generation.

Yes, for your generation, the options are clear—it's either revival or rigor mortis.

What About Manifestations?

And so I sat in the midst of a postmodern Pentecost at the school of ministry, watching God have His way. Using nameless, faceless ones, He spread the fire of revival to over a thousand others. I thought to myself, *The world will beat a path to this place just to receive ten minutes of this outpouring.*

I kept my eyes on the facial expressions of the students. Their faces told it all. Eyes dripped tears, and faces shone with the glory of God. Many were so overcome with the raw power of God's presence that they had to be supported or carried back to their seats. Once they got to their pews, they fell over crying or laughing, pouring out their souls to the Lord. Many rolled onto the floor, trembling under God's power.

As I watched this young generation shaking and quaking in God's presence, I thought of John Wesley's revivals in which sometimes people's "very bones shook."[8] Just as in Wesley's day, people still criticize, saying it's the devil that makes people shake, but we know better.

The way I look at it is like this: in Isaiah's vision of the Temple, the very thresholds shook (see Isaiah 6); when Moses was to receive the Law, the whole mountain quaked (see Exodus 19:18); and when the New Testament Church prayed, the whole room rocked (see Acts 4). So if a temple, a mountain, and a room could shake in the presence of God, why not a mere human frame?

When the Ark of God's presence was returned to Israel, the people who looked inside trembled and shook. Why not? Look in the Bible at all the times people trembled before God, and you'll no longer say it's unscriptural, as some critics contend. The reason they criticize is that they base their judgment on their own lack of experience. When God visits His people in revival, shaking is normal. What else can one do in the presence of a mighty God?

Jonathan Edwards wrote of people who trembled, cried out, wept profusely, leapt for joy, and fainted, or "swooned" with love sickness.[9] Though he insisted that "bodily effects" neither prove nor disprove that a work is from the Spirit of God, his own wife was in a "swoon," or trancelike state, for more than two weeks. She was so overcome with the presence of God that she lost all bodily strength.

Edwards explained that our frail human bodies are not made for overwhelming views of God, such as Daniel, Ezekiel, or the apostle John experienced. Jewish divines, said Edwards, even believed that Moses had such an encounter with God on Mount Nebo that he literally died from the ecstasy of His presence.[10]

When revival swept across the eastern seaboard of America in the first Great Awakening in the 1740s, critics raged against Edwards. His chief opponent, Charles Chauncy, wrote his *Seasonable Thoughts on the State of Religion in New England*, asserting that the "stir in religion" under Edwards (also spread by George Whitefield) was a result of fanatical extravagance.[11]

Chauncy described one of Edwards' meetings as being filled with confusion; some screaming, some praying, others singing or jumping up and down, and some lying prostrate on the floor. He warned of "roarings, tremblings, and the strangest bodily effects which," he insisted, "proved the work could not be of God."[12]

Edwards responded by writing his *Distinguishing Marks of a Work of the Spirit of God.* In this classic work on revival, he showed that revivals must be judged, not by outward manifestations on the body, but by inward responses of the heart. True revival would always result in the fruit of changed lives.[13]

Though he insisted that physical manifestations on human bodies proved nothing, he strongly approved of the manifestations occurring in his own church. In another classic work on revival, Edwards told how he felt about bodily manifestations:

> Now if such things are enthusiasm, and the fruit of a distempered brain, let my brain be forevermore possessed of that happy distemper! If this be distraction, I pray God that the whole world of mankind may be all seized with this benign, meek, beneficent, beatific, glorious distraction![14]

Edwards would never say that bodily manifestations proved or disproved revival. He would simply ask: Do the people now exalt Jesus Christ more highly? Have they withdrawn from the kingdom of darkness? Do they now love the Bible more deeply? Do they appreciate truth more sincerely? Do they love God and others more intensely? If they did, then, Edwards would affirm, the revival was a true work of the Spirit of God.[15]

Is There Any Fruit?[16]

With these thoughts in the back of my mind, I slipped up closer to some of the ones who were vibrating on their seats next to me and listened ...

"Oh, Jesus, Jesus, Jesus, ..." cried a girl next to me.

"I'm so hungry, Lord, I'm so desperate for You, Lord!" cried another.

"O God, forgive me, forgive me. I've backslidden from You," sobbed a boy on his knees.

A young man standing in the front of the sanctuary

lunged back to the front pew. His face was beet red, and his hands trembled. He was totally drunk in the Spirit.[17] I could feel the Holy Spirit emanating from every pore of his being. Suddenly he let out a WHOOP, then stood and wailed in tearful joy.

A young African-American danced with abandon, flailing his arms and hands in the air, joy bursting from his eyes. Another young man threw his arms as wide as he could reach, then bent back almost in a backbend. It was as though he couldn't open wide enough to Heaven's rain, now drenching him.

As I watched the students, I noticed that some seemed to receive more than others. I only know that the more one drinks of the Spirit of God, the deeper one receives. It's just the opposite of drinking in the world, where the more one drinks, the more it takes to get drunk. In the Lord, the more one drinks of the wine of Heaven, the easier it is to get drunk in the Spirit.

I could hardly believe the joy exploding from these young people, but it made sense, because, again, one who is forgiven much loves much. The reason these students burst with such uproarious joy is because they have come so far, they've come from such deep pain, and now their joy is uncontainable.

I thought, *These guys aren't manifesting the flesh or worshiping the devil, as critics would assert. They are totally in love with Jesus Christ.*

And frankly, I know the lives of these young people. Like so many, they have come out of lives of gross sin, but Jesus has washed them, and they are walking in incredible purity. Most of the boys won't even hold a girl's hand or kiss her during their first year at school. They don't want anything to distract them from their call in God, so they are committed to sexual purity on every level.

I have revival students living here at the camp, and every morning I can hear guitars playing, the voices of those who are singing, and students wailing in prayer. Some pray outside in the prayer garden, some pound the heavens in closets, and some pray in prayer rooms. Music fills every corner of the camp, for these young men burn and blaze for Jesus Christ. Their lives display the extraordinary fruit of revival.

"More Fire!"

Finally, my turn came to enter the prayer tunnel. I laid aside my notepad and stood in line, waiting until I thought my heart would burst. As I neared the prayer line, my face burned with the intensity of the heat. I started through the line ... then I stumbled. Someone came behind me and supported me through the line. I looked up and saw young men and women, praying fervently, touching me lightly, as I lurched through the line. I was broken by the words of their prayers:

> "More compassion, Lord!"
> "More wisdom, Lord!"
> "More anointing, Lord! More burden for the lost! More burden for the youth!"
> "More love! More passion, Lord!"
> "More understanding and knowledge, Lord!"
> "More brokenness! ..."

As I neared the end of the line, someone cried, "Fire! More fire!" and I almost passed out. A lady shouldered me to a pew, where I fell over sobbing for joy. There, I cried and prayed and trembled before God.

When I could finally recover myself, I rose and staggered over and around bodies to find my notepad. I wrote, "Jesus, now I know for certain how You will spread revival to this land." I drew in a deep breath and continued:

> As a young generation drinks more and more of Your Spirit, You will heal them and fill them and send them out. Then they will impart the fire of revival to their generation and to the generations to follow. And this nation will burst into flames of revival, as this generation sets *America Ablaze* for Jesus Christ!

Endnotes:

1. Malcolm McDow, "The Southwestern Story," in *Revival!* John Avant, Malcolm McDow, Alvin Reid, eds., (Nashville: Broadman and Holman Publishers, 1996), p. 62.
2. Bill Bright, "Afterword," in *Revival!* John Avant, Malcolm McDow, Alvin Reid, eds. (Nashville: Broadman and Holman Publishers, 1996), p. 176.
3. Malcolm McDow, *Revival!* p. 62.
4. Student testimony from Harvest Rock Church in Pasadena, CA.
5. Donald Cronkite, "Quenching the Spirit or Discerning the Spirits," in *Perspectives* 10(6) 1995, pp. 14-16.
6. Lyle Dorsett, "The Wheaton Revival of 1995: A Chronicle and Assessment", in *Accounts of a Campus Revival, Wheaton College 1995* (Wheaton, IL: Harold Shaw Publishers, 1995), p. 91.
7. Ben Patterson, *Perspectives* 10(6) 1995, p. 16.
8. John Wesley, quoted in Steve Beard, *Thunderstruck: John Wesley and the Toronto Blessing* (Wilmore, KS: Thunderstruck Communications, 1996), p. 6.
9. Jonathan Edwards, "Some Thoughts Concerning the Present Revival of Religion in New England, and the Way It Ought to Be Acknowledged and Promoted," in *The Works of Jonathan Edwards*, Vol. 1, 9th edition, pp. 365-430 (Edinburgh: Banner of Truth Trust, 1995), p. 376.

10. Interestingly, in tracing Charles Chauncy's influence in history, according to Ian Murray, his work eventually evolved into Unitarianism and universalism (Ian Murray, *Jonathan Edwards: A New Biography* [Edinburgh: Banner of Truth Trust, 1996], p. 454). On the other hand, the influence of Jonathan Edwards on evangelical theology still lives on today. He is considered "preeminently the theologian of Revival, the theologian of experience, or as some have put it, the theologian of the heart," said D. Martyn Lloyd-Jones (Lloyd-Jones, *The Puritans* [Westchester, PA: Banner of Truth Trust, 1987], p. 361).

11. Ian Murray, *Jonathan Edwards: A New Biography*, pp. 336-369.

12. Charles Chauncy, *Seasonable Thoughts on the State of Religion in New England* (Boston, MA: Rogers and Fowle, 1743), p. 6.

13. Jonathan Edwards, "An Account of the Revival of Religion in Northampton, 1740-1742," in *Jonathan Edwards on Revival* (Edinburgh: Banner of Truth Trust, pp. 89-90.

14. Jonathan Edwards, *The Works of Jonathan Edwards,* Vol. 1, 9th edition, p. 376. Sadly, several modern-day Charles Chauncys have condemned the work of God in revival today. Many of them grossly misquote Jonathan Edwards' theology, revising history to falsely support their views. A large portion of my Ph.D. dissertation for Fuller Theological Seminary was on the theology of Jonathan Edwards. My spirit grieves as I've read the writings of these men, claiming to speak for the Orthodox Christian faith. They have twisted Edwards and completely misrepresented his thoughts.

15. Jonathan Edwards, *Distinguishing Marks of a Work of the Spirit of God,* in *Jonathan Edwards on Revival,* pp. 75-147 (Edinburgh: Banner of Truth Trust, 1995).

16. After sending questionnaires through the nation to postmodern students of college age who had participated in revival in 1995, I found that seventy-five percent of them had answered a call into ministry. A student from Hope College told me, "I work in the recruitment department of my seminary part-time now, and the number of students moved to ministry by these revivals is astounding" (testimony from Wheaton College, 1998). That's what I call "fruit." Out of all the groups I researched from twelve colleges and college-age groups, eighty-seven percent were now helping the poor and winning souls, which I think is fantastic. This shows again why revival meets the challenge of postmodernity, but even more—revival transforms young lives and compels them to do exploits for God.

17. If being drunk in the Spirit offends you, read about respected Methodist missionary E. Stanley Jones being drunk in the Lord for days (in Chapter 7).

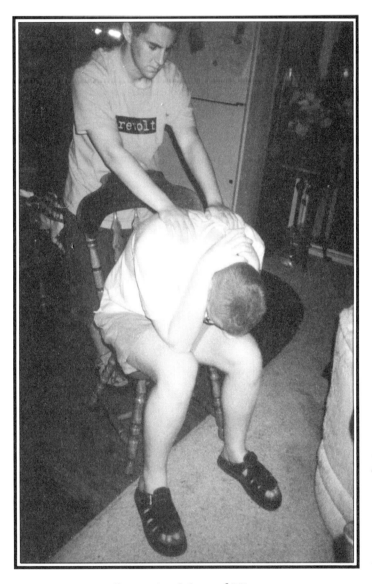

Imparting More of Him

The
Bloodstained
Torch

Carry the Torch for Your Generation

Chapter 6

The Bloodstained Torch

On a sunny April morning in Colorado, a beautiful teenager sits outside a school cafeteria, chatting with a friend. Suddenly, two wild-eyed students approach, carrying pipe bombs and guns. They laugh as they spray the two innocent kids with a barrage of bullets.

One of the victims, Richard Castaldo, breaks into a run, but nine more bullets mow him down. The girl falls to the ground, hit in the leg, chest, and arm. While she is lying there in a pool of blood, one of the killers grabs her by the hair and shouts in her face, "Do you still believe in God now?" Through her pain, she cries, "You know I do!" "Then go be with Him!" he snarls, squeezing the trigger and blowing Rachel Joy Scott into the arms of Jesus.[1]

Later, through gut-wrenching sobs, Rachel's brother Craig tells his story. He and his two friends, Isaiah Shoels and Matt Kechter, are sitting in the library when they hear shouts about gunmen shooting up the school. They dive under a table and hide, just as the killers burst into the library.

After blasting several kids, one of the murderers eyes a black student hiding under a table. "Hey, there's a n_____ under here!" he sneers. Isaiah Shoels keeps silent as bullets tear into his body, and he dies. Next, the shooters open fire on Matt Kechter, and suddenly Craig finds himself in puddles of his own friends' blood. He tries to play dead, while experiencing the horror of hearing his two friends gasping and dying beside him.[2]

Cassie Bernall has been sitting in the library reading her Bible. When the killers storm into the library, Cassie prays fervently. One of the gunmen asks, "Do you believe in God?" According to several students, Cassie responds, "Yes, I do believe in God!" and she is instantly shot to death.[3]

At the same time, Valeen Schnurr also ducks beneath a table, holding her best friend Lauren Townsend's hand. Suddenly a pipe bomb explodes, and the murderers pepper that area of the library with bullets. Valeen clutches her stomach, as multiple bullets and shrapnel pump into her body. "Oh, my God! Oh, my God!" she cries in pain.

"God?" snorts one of the killers, hearing her cry. "Do you believe in God?"

Valeen later tells her mother that she was afraid to say yes, and afraid to say no because she believed she was dying.

Finally, she musters the courage to say, "Yes, I believe in God."

"Why?" asks one of the killers as he reloads his gun.

"My parents brought me up that way, and I believe," she answers. She still doesn't understand why the gunmen walk away. But as they leave the room, she turns to her friend, whose hand she still holds, and reaches up to touch her face. "Wake up, Lauren, it's time to get out," she whispers. She struggles to get her friend to safety, but then she realizes—Lauren is gone.[4]

At this point, Craig Scott distinctly recalls hearing the voice of God say, "Get up and get out now!" He leaps to his feet and surveys the carnage around him. Seeing Kasey Ruegsegger, with her shoulder bone sticking out and her arm almost blown off, he grabs her. Blood covers both of them, as Craig gently cradles her arm and helps her to safety. He comes back and helps other kids out of the blood-splattered library, all the while searching the rubble of the school for his sister. He even prays with friends to find their own brothers and sisters, but he says, "I just couldn't find Rachel anywhere!"[5]

That day, April 20, 1999, was a turning point in American history.[6] As human blood spilled onto the floor of a public high school, God looked down and saw it all. If the blood of Abel cried out to God from the ground (see Genesis 4:10), how much more the blood of these postmodern American martyrs.

Tertullian said, "The blood of the martyrs is the seed of the church." In the year 2000 alone, there were a hundred and sixty-five thousand Christians martyred for their faith, but these deaths occurred outside of America.[7] "Now today," says Tommy Tenney, "It's not just martyrs' blood, it's *our* martyrs' blood."[8]

"There is a sound crying out from Columbine High School right now," proclaimed Cindy Jacobs when she spoke at the Brownsville Revival in late September of 2000. "It's the sound of the martyrs."[9]

A National Challenge

Just before the first rays of the new millennium burst across the horizon of time, this national tragedy awakened the soul of the nation. As Lou Engle said, "It was a defining moment" in America's history.[10] In his book *The Martyrs' Torch*, Bruce Porter, who preached Rachel Scott's funeral, wrote:

> It has become something of a spiritual "Pearl Harbor" experience for the Body of Christ in America. As a people, we are being shaken out of our lethargy, complacency, and indifference by this vicious carnage. This is nowhere more evident than in the youth. We are witnessing the birth of a national reformation among young lives.[11]

Pastor Lou Engle wrote, "In the midst of an unparalleled assault on this generation, God is recruiting an army of recklessly abandoned youth, completely devoted to Himself." He explains, "There is a new breed of youth arising, who know what it is to love much because they have been forgiven much."[12]

Pastor Porter, after sorting through the rubble and carnage and heartache of Columbine, issued a gripping challenge at Rachel's funeral. Before a sea of three thousand, mostly young, faces in Littleton, and before untold millions around the world listening to the service carried on CNN, he said:

She was a warrior, but she didn't fight her war with guns and with instruments of destruction. Rachel fought with the implements of love and compassion and caring and mercy. ... But as a warrior, Rachel carried a torch that was stained by the blood of the martyrs from the very first day of the Church's existence. ...

Rachel carried a torch—a torch of truth, a torch of compassion, a torch of love, a torch of the good news of Jesus Christ her Lord, whom she was not ashamed of, even in her hour of death. I want to lay a challenge before each and every one of you young people here today: The torch has fallen from Rachel's hand. Who will pick it up again? ...

I want to know right now who will take up that torch. Let me see you. Stand up. Who will pick up Rachel's torch? Who will do it? Hold it high![13]

Suddenly, hundreds of young men and women shot to their feet, as the auditorium exploded in applause. Pastor Porter later learned that thousands of young people had leapt to their feet all over the world, pledging to grip the fallen torch.[14]

Later, a prophetic vision and word came to Pastor Porter from Jim Paul in Ontario, who had been watching the funeral on CNN:

As I watched Rachel's white casket, ... I saw the casket become very large, and it was covered still with signatures—thousands of them this time—but they were prayers for young people. Believers all over the world were interceding for this young generation that is on the brink of burial. All of a sudden an explosion took place, the casket flew open, and a whole generation of young people came to life and poured out. A revival of youth is imminent![15]

This same man went on to say that Stephen's blood thrust Saul into the "arms of God and then into the greatest revival and apostolic ministry that the world had seen." In the same way, "a revival amongst young people has now been released by this fresh blood of young martyrs."[16]

Yes, it's time. A revival has begun, catapulting a young generation into the center of God's plan for this country. I believe it will result in a Third Great Awakening in America. It will bring about a transformation of this nation. In the words of Rachel's dad, Darrell Scott: "There is a spiritual awakening taking place that will not be squelched."[17] Pastor Porter wrote:

It is my firm belief that God is sovereignly moving by His mighty Spirit upon this generation of young people. I believe that we are about to witness the greatest ingathering of people to Christ ever witnessed since the Church was brought forth upon the earth.[18]

A few months after the Columbine tragedy, a thousand young men and women from twenty-eight states and several nations poured into Littleton, Colorado, for the first Torchgrab rally. There, just a few miles from Columbine High School, loud cries for a national revival filled the air. Worship exploded and "heart-wrenching weeping over a lost generation" pierced the heavens. The day was concluded with a challenge once again to take up the bloodstained torch of the fallen Columbine martyrs.[19]

After this, scores of Torchgrab rallies broke out all across the nation. In San Francisco, sixteen thousand people gathered to hear the message of hope for a wounded generation. Ron Luce of Teen Mania's "Acquire the Fire" held a gathering in Detroit shortly after Columbine, with seventy-three thousand teens. In an article for *Charisma* magazine in 1999, Luce said, "We've produced a generation of broken hearts."[20]

At "The Call DC," on September 2, 2000, more than three hundred thousand young people gathered on the Washington Mall. With indescribable passion, Lou Engle, in his inimitable roar, called young men and women to a forty-day fast. Then he urged them to cry out to God for fire:

> Lift your voices and pray, "O Lord God of Abraham, Isaac, and Jacob, George Washington, Jonathan Edwards, Charles Finney, answer again by fire in America. Send the fire today, all over the land. Send the fire of conviction of sin!"

"Let the rains of revival come!" cried a young man at The Call. "Lord, we want to see your face. O God, we're hungry. We're desperate. There's a longing in our hearts that we can't quench!" The crowd exploded with life, responding to every message and prayer. I had never seen so much passion in my life, and I believe The Call will swell and increase and spread revival to youth all across America.

Standing Up for Jesus

Lou Engle tells about a public high school in Tennessee in the wake of the Columbine tragedy. The principal, moved by the events in Littleton, Colorado, invited a Baptist pastor to speak to the entire school on closed-circuit TV. That pastor preached a bold Gospel message, challenging students to stand up in front of their friends, even as Cassie and Rachel stood up in front of the barrel of a gun. He invited those who wanted to accept Christ to come to the media center. Doors opened and students spilled out of classrooms. More than a hundred students prayed to receive Christ that day, and that took place in one of our public schools.[21]

Eight months after Columbine, while I was still in Texas, I, too, became emboldened to take a stand in the public schools. We had been bringing food and Christmas gifts to a school for pregnant Hispanic and African-American girls for six years, always giving the Gospel message and a call to receive Christ. Each year ten or fifteen girls had received the Lord.

But in the aftermath of Columbine, we decided to take

a more radical approach. This time, as we entered the public school, I came armed with a baptism video from the Brownsville Revival. After feeding about sixty girls and thirty babies—with chicken, assorted vegetables, potato casserole, rolls, chocolate éclair cake, and more—we showered them with gifts. Then we showed the video.

As the girls watched other teens standing in the baptismal waters, they realized that these were people just like them—pregnant, abused and dumped by boyfriends, addicted to drugs, sex, and alcohol—who now trembled under the power of God. As the teens at Brownsville had gone under the waters of baptism, many of them had been so overcome by the presence of God they had to be carried out by several strong men.

I looked around the school cafeteria and saw those street-toughened girls sniffing and wiping away tears. The presence of God filled the room. Then I stood and gave a bold altar call, inviting them to come and receive Jesus Christ. Out of sixty teenagers, at least fifty-five stood and sincerely accepted Jesus Christ as their Savior. And it all happened in a public school.

Some would say that I was taking a big risk, but what did I have to lose? My reputation? I lost that years ago. Jail? What I was doing was not illegal, but even if it had been, would it be so bad to go to jail for Jesus?

Richard Wurmbrand, who spent fourteen years in a Romanian prison camp for refusing to deny Christ, asks the American Church a penetrating question: "When the Supreme Court outlawed prayer in public schools in 1962, why did you obey?"[22] Wurmbrand's question pierces straight to the heart of the issue, for after Columbine—after the shedding of martyrs' blood on American soil—we dare not place the law of man above the law of God.

Pastor Richard Crisco has never been afraid to lead His young people in a stand for Christ. When revival hit Brownsville in 1995, Crisco challenged them. At the end of three months of revival, just before school started, he said, "I have watched you shake and tremble and cry for the past three months. Now, I want to see you shake your schools. God has touched you; now I want to see you touch the world."[23]

During that year's high school football season, Crisco's youth took signs to the school game. Someone blew a whistle before each game, and the Brownsville kids came marching in, lifting their signs and praying the Lord's Prayer. The cheerleaders helped lead the prayer, and when school officials chastised them for it, the mothers of the cheerleaders chimed in, "Okay, if you won't let them do it, we'll lead the prayer at the next game!"

At another school, this one in Hattiesburg, Mississippi, students again defied the ruling outlawing school prayer at football games. Before the game, they stood together and prayed the Lord's Prayer.[24]

The question Richard Wurmbrand posed so eloquently still pierces us with conviction: "When the Supreme Court outlawed prayer in the schools, why did you obey?" Even more, the words of Rachel and Cassie ring in our hearts—"Yes, I believe in God!" This is our rallying cry. The time to stand up for what we believe is now.

What Are Your Rights?

In fact, most of you probably don't really know what your rights are in a public school. You've been intimidated into believing it is unlawful to take a Bible or talk about your faith. This is not true.

In 1984, Ronald Reagan signed the Equal Access Act into law. A portion of that law gives freedom to express one's religious beliefs on a public school campus. You have the freedom to meet with other students to discuss religious issues. You have the fundamental freedom to talk about your faith on campus. You can even pray on campus, by yourself or with others, as long as you don't force your prayer on others and you don't disrupt school activities.

The Supreme Court has said that "only state-directed Bible reading is unconstitutional," so you have the right to read your Bible at school. You also have the right to do research papers, speeches, and projects with "religious themes."[25]

For too long we've been intimidated by those who have been operating out of their own fears or religious unbelief. It's time to throw open the windows and openly pray as Daniel did—even if it means being thrown into the lions' den. It's time to stand up for Jesus and against authorities, as Peter and John did—even if it means being thrown into jail.

In one American public school, confession of sin actually broke out during an assembly. The principal chose to let the confession continue all day. Later, she received criticism, but she also received much appreciation. One father wrote, "Thank you for your courage. You have done the equivalent of not moving to the back of the bus."[26]

Yes, if the Civil Rights Movement brought needed change in America when Rosa Parks was willing to go to jail before she would give up her seat to a white man, why can't we stand up for our cause? Martin Luther King, Jr., was willing to spill his blood for his grand dream, and we can do no less—if it comes to that—for the young men and women of our nation and for the cause of our Lord Jesus Christ.

Rachel Scott's dad, Darrell Scott, wrote this poem, which he read to the Subcommittee on Crime in the United States House of Representatives:

> Your laws ignore our deepest needs,
> Your words are empty air,
> You've stripped away our heritage,
> You've outlawed simple prayer.
> Now, gunshots fill our classrooms
> And precious children die.
> You seek for answers everywhere,
> And ask the question "WHY?"
> You regulate restrictive laws
> Through legislative creed,
> And yet you fail to understand
> That God is what we need.[27]

Will You Take Up the Torch?

Yes, a bloodstained torch is passing down from Columbine's martyrs to a whole generation. This past summer, at our revival camp, I saw how quickly the Lord breathed revival down on those who were hungry.

Praise had barely begun on the second night when the spirit of revival burst through the room, and everyone instantly caught the blaze. One particularly hard-hearted boy saw a friend melting under the Holy Spirit's conviction, so he ran upstairs to avoid the heat of God's presence. Later he admitted, "I couldn't get away from the presence of God, as hard as I tried! I ran upstairs and cried and cried, because I was so angry over what I had done with my life."

Meanwhile, the members of his youth group were downstairs lifting their hands up, roaring to God in prayer for his salvation. By the third night, a tall, good-looking seventeen-year-old, who had come to camp because his parents forced him to, melted before the Lord. Now he carries the torch of revival to his church and city and school.

That's what it's all about. One person who carries fire touches another and another ... until finally America blazes with revival.

Reach Up to Jesus

Now, God calls you to step up and grip the torch for your generation. Will you be part of this torch-bearing throng? If you say *yes*, then pause now and look up to Jesus. His eyes search the nation, looking for those who will take the torch, which the Columbine martyrs dropped. So fix your gaze on Him. See Him seated on the throne, looking down on you. Look now at the pierced hand that holds the flaming torch. He shed His blood and drank the Father's cup of fiery wrath so that He could hand this torch of fire to you.

If you are willing to be a "living martyr" on earth, if you are willing to boldly witness for Jesus—even if it means being unpopular or persecuted and rejected for the Lord Jesus—then reach up now and grasp with all your might the bloodstained torch.

Endnotes:

1. Bruce Porter, *The Martyrs' Torch: The Message of the Columbine Massacre* (Shippensburg, PA: Destiny Image Publishers, Inc., 1999), p. 1, 53.
   Pastor Bruce Porter says that the stories about Rachel's, Cassie's, and others' last words are unsubstantiated, but this is what some believe they said.
2. Bruce Porter, *The Martyrs' Torch*, pp. 6-7.
3. Bruce Porter, *The Martyrs' Torch*, p. 6.
4. Bruce Porter, *The Martyrs' Torch*, pp. 7-8.
5. Bruce Porter, *The Martyrs' Torch*, pp. 9-11.
6. From 1992-1999, two hundred and fifty-three students have been killed in school-associated violence. Though we consider Columbine as the worst school shooting in American history, in 1927 forty-five people were slaughtered at the Consolidated School in Bath, Michigan (Curtis Esquibel, "School Violence Far From New," *Denver Post Online*, April 24, 1999).
   The University of Denver's Carl Raschke, professor of religious studies, said that the fact that the Columbine massacre fell on the birthday of Adolph Hitler "probably explains a lot more than we can imagine." He told the *Denver Post*, "They want to honor the memory of the master, and these kids seriously look to Hitler the same way young blacks look to Martin Luther King and the way many Christians look to Jesus" (quoted by Susan Green and Bill Briggs, "Massacre at Columbine High: Attention Focuses on 'Trench Coat Mafia,'" *Denver Post Online*, April 21, 1999.
7. David Barrett, "Status of Global Mission, 2001, in Context of 20th and 21st Centuries," in *The Global Evangelization Movement*, www.gem-werc.org/, p. 1.
8. Tommy Tenny, endorsements, in Bruce Porter, *The Martyrs' Torch*, p. vii.
9. Cindy Jacobs, in a message at Brownsville Assembly of God, Pensacola, FL, September 2000.
10. Lou Engle, *Fast Forward: A Call to the Millennial Prayer Revolution* (Pasadena, CA: cu@dc, 1999), p. 1.
    Just twenty days before the Columbine massacre, Cindy Jacobs had given a prophetic word to the pastors in the Denver area, warning them to pray for every city in the area. The Lord had told her: "America will pay for its godlessness with the lives of its children" (told by Jacobs to the Brownsville Assembly of God Church, September 30, 2000).
11. Bruce Porter, *The Martyrs' Torch*, p. xxiii.

12. Lou Engle, *Fast Forward,* p. 10.
13. Bruce Porter, *The Martyrs' Torch,* pp. 34-35.
14. Ibid., p. 52.
15. Jim Paul, East Gate Christian Fellowship, Hamilton, Ontario; quoted in Bruce Porter, *The Martyrs' Torch,* p. 39.
16. Jim Paul, *The Martyrs' Torch,* pp. 39-40.
17. Darrell Scott, quoted in Bruce Porter, *The Martyrs' Torch,* p. 66.
18. Bruce Porter, *The Martyrs' Torch,* p. 91.
19. Claudia Porter, quoted in Bruce Porter, *The Martyrs' Torch,* pp. 86-87. See www.torchgrab.org
20. Ron Luce, "The Cry of a Lost Generation," *Charisma* magazine (September, 1999), p. 49, quoted in Bruce Porter, *The Martyrs' Torch,* p. 84.
21. Lou Engle, *Fast Forward,* p. 4.
22. Richard Wurmbrand, *Tortured for Christ*; quoted by Michael Brown in *Revolution* (Ventura, CA: Renew, 2000), p. 54.
23. Richard Crisco, *It's Time*, p. 94.
24. Told by Cindy Jacobs while preaching at Brownsville in late September 2000.
25. This is called "The Students' Bill of Rights on a Public School Campus." It is published by J.W. Brinkley and Roever Communications (P.O. Box 136130, Ft. Worth, TX, 76136, phone: 817-238-2005. For more information see *Students LEGAL RIGHTS on a Public School Campus*, which may be obtained by calling or writing the National Youth Alive Office, 1445 Boonville Ave., Springfield, MO 65802, phone: 800-545-2766).
26. Michael Brown, "Jesus Manifesto," p. 5, originally from *Time*, June 5, 2000, p. 61.
27. Cited in Lou Engle, *Fast Forward: A Call to the Millennial Prayer Revolution* (Pasadena, CA: cu@dc, 1999),p. 68. Lou Engle issued this call to extreme commitment:
"Young man, young woman, you may think you're insignificant, but you were born in maybe the most extraordinary generation of history. Your generation was created by God with the DNA of extremism. ... He wants to turn that to an extreme holy love of God, the John the Baptist generation of whom the Bible said, *'From the age of John the Baptist the kingdom of heaven suffers violence and the violent take it by force.'* Not a violence of anger, but a violence of love, of fasting, and prayer. You can be a history maker. Don't watch history pass you by. Make history. Lead the parade of history" (Lou Engle, "Highlights From The Call," a video from 1539 E. Howard St., Pasadena, CA, order from www.elijahrevolution.com).

Camp America Ablaze Photo

Ministering to Your Own Generation

Campus
Ablaze

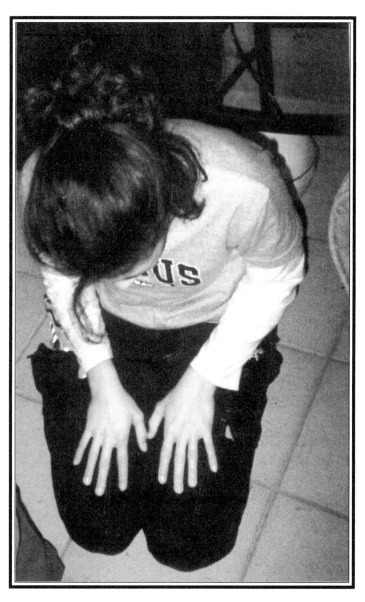

Broken Before Him

Chapter 7

Campus Ablaze

I believe that Jesus looks down over America and yearns over your generation. He scans the country and sees young men and women, hearts boiling with revival, flames of passion leaping from the altar of your hearts. He sees the tears of love and hears the abandoned worship. But He also sees those who still don't know Him. He looks inside a typical postmodern college campus, and His heart aches over what He sees there.

The American Campus

Our Lord hears young men boasting of their sexual conquests over the weekend. He listens to them laugh about how drunk or stoned they were. But He looks beneath the surface and sees into their hearts. He feels the pain, the confusion, the loneliness, the anger.

He looks into their empty souls and sees how meaningless life is for them. He sees how spiritual they are, but He also knows how they detest the hype, hypocrisy, and materialism of the baby boomer church of their parents. He understands how they long for something real, something genuine and authentic in which they can believe.

If you are a college student reading these pages, you may feel quite alone on your campus. If you're on a secular campus, it probably seems rather hopeless. Even if you're on a Christian campus, you may not be experiencing the full flood of Heaven-sent revival.

I believe Jesus looks down now and longs to breathe across your campus. He yearns to open the wound in His heart and send down a river over you. He has always delighted in sending revival to the young. He will send it to your school—if you will prepare the way.

Come with me now to glimpse special seasons of revival on America campuses. Discover what moves God's heart and causes Him to send down a deluge of His Spirit.

American Campus Revivals of the Past

Slip with me inside a dormitory at Hampton-Sydney College in 1787.[1] Hear four young men praying their hearts out, while angry students pound on their door, yelling threats and curses, demanding that they stop praying. Not until a professor breaks up the mob does the rioting cease.

When college president John B. Smith hears the story, he looks at the boys with tears in his eyes. "My dear young friends, you shall be protected," he says. "You shall hold your next meeting in my parlor, and I will be one of your number."[2]

114

With this support, curious students begin attending the prayer meetings, and soon the whole campus is caught up in a revival. In fact, visitors tell of experiencing the power of the Holy Spirit as soon as they come across the county line. Those who come to the revival take the fire home to their own churches, and soon revival spreads.[3]

Look now beside a river outside Williams College in 1806. See five young men praying in a maple grove, away from campus to avoid persecution. Once again, the Lord hears a cry piercing the heavenlies, as they plead for revival and world missions.

Suddenly a storm bursts through the skies, and the young men dive into a haystack, still praying. God hears their prayers and breathes across their campus, sweeping Williams College, and soon many other campuses, with revival. Clarence Shedd wrote in *Two Centuries of Student Christian Movements*, "The lighted torch passed on by the Haystack Group ... set aflame the missionary passion of the American church."[4]

But, by the mid 1850s, sororities and fraternities had sprung up on college campuses, emphasizing social and worldly activities, rather than spiritual and academic pursuits. The modern era—"modernity"—was in full force, and slavery scarred the soul of the nation. By now, students rebelled against compulsory prayer and chapel.[5] At Williams College, where the Haystack Revival had broken out, students spat on the floor during chapel and wrote obscene words in hymnals.

Then, at Princeton in 1879, a young man, Luther Wishard, began to pray for revival. As head of a campus ministry, he planned a series of meetings with D.L. Moody. Moody had been saved in 1856 and ignited with fervor during the great prayer revival of 1857. God used Moody to ignite one of the greatest revivals in the history of Princeton. By the scores, students came asking, "What must I do to be saved?"[6] Yet it all began because a young man, Luther Wishard, lifted his heart to Heaven and prayed.

This is just what God was waiting to hear. He wanted to hear the prayers of a student crying out to Him for revival on a college campus. This is why I want to encourage you college students who are desperate for a move of God, to pray for your campus to be ablaze with revival.

Twentieth-Century Campus Revivals

Now, let's consider what God did in the twentieth century on college campuses. I believe those campus revivals were forerunners to the outpouring of national revival He wants to give today.

As the twentieth century dawned, the modern era rose to a peak, with the secular and atheistic teachings of Friedrich Nietzsche, Karl Marx, Sigmund Freud, and Charles Darwin. In the midst of this darkness, however, God began to breathe revival on Wales, and soon after, on Americans at Azusa Street in Los Angeles. But He also had His eyes upon some college boys, at a little school nestled among the hills of Kentucky. It all started in 1905 at Asbury College, as five students prayed in a dorm room.

Later, E. Stanley Jones wrote, "Suddenly we were all

swept off our feet by a visitation of the Holy Spirit. We were all filled, flooded by the Spirit. ... Everything that happened to the disciples on the original Pentecost happened to us. For three or four days it could be said of us as was said of those at the original Pentecost, 'They are drunk.' I was drunk with God."[7]

By the next morning the powerful influence of this sudden outpouring had spread over the whole campus. Students prostrated themselves in prayer during chapel, and for three days every classroom was a prayer meeting. It spread to the countryside, and people flocked to the campus. Jones said that before people could get inside the auditorium they "would be stricken with conviction and would fall on their knees on the campus crying for God—and pardon and release."

Jones, who became a Methodist missionary to India, later recalled that this revival "was the cleanest, least maneuvered, the most 'untouched-by-human-hands,' the most constructive and spiritually and morally productive movement I have ever seen."[9] During that same year, signs of revival swept college campuses throughout the whole nation, for God was breathing on students.[9]

Let these facts encourage your heart, young man or woman, for you are living in the day when, as never before, God is breathing down from Heaven on your generation. Right now, you are in a prime position as a missionary to your campus.

Let God give you a burden for students in your school. Then join with others to pray earnestly and passionately for revival. As surely as He sent it when students prayed at Williams or Princeton or Asbury, He will send revival to your campus as well. Remember, He wants revival even more than you do.

This is what happened at Wheaton College in 1936 and 1943, and again in 1950, while the nation was recovering from the Second World War. During a chapel service, a professor humbled himself and repented to the students for slandering another professor. This broke the students. Several responded with testimonies, and the Holy Spirit moved over everyone present.

A few nights later, students packed the chapel to unburden their souls. Confession lasted on through the night and the rest of the week. *Life* magazine reported, "College Revival Becomes Confession Marathon."[10] As a result of that revival, over thirty-nine percent of the graduating class of the college gave their lives to full-time missions or other ministries.[11]

A few weeks after this outbreak at Wheaton, a student named Bob Barefoot, who was consumed with a passion for souls, began earnestly praying for a revival again at Asbury. One night he prayed with several students to receive Christ.

The next morning in chapel, he told about the students being saved. Suddenly, winds of the Spirit blew into Hughes Auditorium. Dee Cobb, the chapel speaker, said it was as though "an electric shock moved over the whole place, and there was such a presence of God that one felt as though he could just reach out and touch Him."[12]

Twenty years later, in 1970, at the height of the counter-cultural hippie movement, as students burned draft cards and locked college presidents in their offices, a small band of students at Asbury gathered to pray for another revival. It came during chapel one morning as the altar was opened. Suddenly, the Holy Spirit swept across the student body, and soon young men and women streamed forward, weeping, repenting, and confessing their sin. One student picked up his pen and wrote:

> I sit in the middle of a contemporary Pentecost. A few moments ago there came a spontaneous movement of the Holy Spirit. I have never witnessed such a mighty outpouring of God upon His people. The scene is unbelievable. The altar has been flooding with needy souls time and time again.[13]

The revival lasted for days, and when spring break came, students fanned out across the nation, telling their stories. At least a hundred and thirty campuses were touched by the 1970 Asbury Revival, and always the fire came because students prayed.[14]

"God Uses Students"

I sat one day in 1988 in the office of Dennis Kinlaw, who had been president of Asbury College during that 1970 Asbury Revival. "Why Asbury? Why this little college hidden in the hills amidst the tobacco farms and horse ranches of Kentucky, rather than some larger, more noted church or institution?" I asked him.

Kinlaw leaned forward, eyes sparkling and face glowing. "It's *students*, Sandy. God uses *students!*"

David McKenna, former president of Asbury Seminary, gave this insight about God using students:

> When God's Spirit is poured out on all people, it is no accident that the young see visions. Nor is it an accident when the stirring of the Spirit that leads to a Great Awakening begins on the college campus. Youth is a choice time of life when special gifts are in full bloom. Never again will a person be so sensitive to cultural conflict, so optimistic about the future, so open to the Spirit, so energized for action, and so ready to die for Christ.[15]

In fact, Jonathan Edwards said, the First Great Awakening was "chiefly amongst the young; and comparatively but few others have been made partakers of it." He warned that "when God has begun any great work for the revival of his church; he has taken the young people, and has cast off the old and stiff-necked generation." The reason, he said, was because of their "obstinate attitude" against an outpouring of God's Spirit.[16]

I'm not suggesting, and I'm sure Edwards was not suggesting, that older adults won't be used in revival. Adults bring wisdom and life experience that help the younger generation. Mike and Cindy Jacobs' son has said that the young generation is like a river, bursting its banks and flooding the land with uncontrollable passion, but the older generation is like the banks of the river, guiding that river, steering it into healthy channels.[17]

I am suggesting that God often uses the young to spearhead revivals, and I believe He will use your generation for the coming floods of worldwide revival.

Revival—Just Before Dawn

Now, let's look at the present day to see what God has been doing to prepare for these coming floods. As the sun began to set on the twentieth century, God started to breathe again from Heaven. He was preparing for a third millennium, or third day, of Christian influence in the earth. After all, Jesus rose on the third day, just before dawn.

By 1995, He had already been pouring out revival on Argentina, on Toronto, and on the meetings of Rodney Howard-Browne in America. Even before the revival broke out in Pensacola, something happened in a little college campus in Brownwood, Texas.

Students there had been seeking God for revival all semester. One Sunday morning, a young man named Chris Robeson entered Coggin Avenue Baptist Church and the Holy Spirit fell on him. A spirit of repentance broke over him as he staggered to the altar to confess his sin to the pastor. I'll let him tell you what happened next:

> It is a miracle that my pastor understood what I said. By this time, I had begun to shake tremendously. I stood before the church and

turned to Joel 2:12. ... I gathered my emotions and shared what I believed to be God's Word to all of us: *"Rend your hearts!"* It has become clear to me that God was desiring to show us just how far away from Him our hearts had gone.[18]

Soon the altar filled with college students as well as adults, weeping in repentance and brokenness. The move of God rapidly spread to the campus at Howard Payne University, and within days, while Henry Blackaby preached a series of messages, six hundred students streamed to the altar to publicly confess their sins. Blackaby said, "Most who were in His presence absolutely could not stand without instantly confessing enormous sin."[19]

News spread quickly, and Howard Payne students were invited to many other campuses to tell their stories. "When you hear that revival has broken loose, you either go where it is or bring it where you are," said one professor.[20] Timothy Beougher, professor at Wheaton, explained that prayer and preparation "stacks the kindling," but God often uses an outsider to bring the "spark" to light the fire.[21]

Soon sparks were flying at Wheaton in a revival that lasted several days. On the last night, an Indonesian graduate student, Leo Somule, whose parents had been saved through American missionaries, challenged the students. He urged them to finish the task of world evangelism, which the 1950 graduating class, also touched by revival, had begun. After an altar call, hundreds rushed forward to commit their lives to full-time missionary service.[22]

On through America the revival spread—from Wheaton, to Asbury, to George Fox, to Messiah College, to Hope College, to Eastern Nazarene, and to many more.

During this time, I was working on my Ph.D. dissertation for Fuller Theological Seminary, and I was seeking to find the answer to the question: How can the Gospel be brought to postmodern generations? I knew in my heart that revival was the answer, but I had to prove objectively that fruit comes from revival.[23] (Please see the Appendix on page 185 for the results.)

I developed a questionnaire based on the marks of revival laid out by Jonathan Edwards, Charles Finney, and John Wesley,[24] and I sent it to college-age students throughout America who had experienced revival in 1995. Gathering the raw data and running "frequency reports," I found that students touched by revival had developed marvelous fruit as a result of revival.

A Strategy for Campus Revival

Now, I want to talk to you about how you can actually be used to bring revival to *your* campus. Do you remember the story of Luther Wishard, the young man at the Princeton Revival?[25] He was president of the Philadelphian Society, a Christian campus organization which later merged with the Young Men's Christian Association.[26] Because he headed up this group, he was in a position to invite an evangelist to the campus to spark a revival.

Here's my challenge to you: If you could start your own student-led revival organization, you would be in a position to invite revivalists to help light the flame on your campus. Why start a new organization? Because it's difficult to put new wine into old wineskins. You need a new student-led campus club, one where the Holy Spirit can freely move in revival.

If you sense that your Christian group would truly welcome revival, even if it comes with unusual manifestations, stay with it. There's no need to reinvent the wheel. But by experience I can tell you that to try to bring revival where the current leadership is not hungry for it, will not work. Your efforts will likely be shut down. That's why I suggest a new wineskin to hold the bubbling new wine of revival. Since "9-11," everything in America has changed. We must have radical, open, passionate, Holy Ghost revival!

A campus group that does hunger for revival is Chi Alpha, backed by the Assemblies of God. If you are interested in starting a Chi Alpha club at your college, or perhaps even becoming a campus pastor, check their website for information.[27] I would also encourage you to come to BRSM to receive training to become a campus minister.

Here at BRSM we have teams of students who carry revival fire. They would gladly come to your campus to help impart revival. You could invite these young firebrands from the Brownsville Revival to come for a few days to preach, prophesy, pray, and impart fire to the students. This would most likely ignite revival on your campus and help your campus group win souls to Jesus Christ.

To further encourage revival among college and high school students, we are inviting you to come out, during spring and summer breaks, to our Camp America Ablaze. We want to give you a chance to drink from the streams of revival and then take it back to your campuses. Our slogan is: "Set the campus ablaze today; set America ablaze tomorrow!" (See our website: www.revivalcamp.com).

Spring Break Ablaze

During our "Spring Break Ablaze" this year, college students came from around the nation. I watched young men and women thundering in prayer over one another. At one point, the Holy Spirit came down in such power that they pounded the floor, crying out in loud sobs to God, pleading for revival in their churches and schools back home. They begged God for holiness of heart. They roared to Him for more. Their hunger burned unbearably deep as they cried, "Here I am, Lord. Use me!"

I watched a young woman lay her hand on the forehead of one of the guys, praying, prophesying, and pouring out her heart. He cried and wailed under the anointing of her prayers. A young man, whose prophetic gift had lain virtually dormant until then, exploded in prophecy, and fresh encouragement filled every heart. Another boy quietly sang a love song to Jesus as though he was the only one in the room.

"Cry out to Him!" urged a young lady. "Don't be ashamed to cry out to Him. He's waiting for you!"

Another boy lay on his back, tears streaming down his temples and soaking into the carpet.

It thrilled my heart to watch, for we long to see young men and women go back home, spreading revival fire to their schools, churches, and college campuses   setting *America Ablaze* for God.

Cry for Revival

Young man or young woman, you were born for revival. God has targeted your generation. He looks down with a pent-up river surging in His breast. Charles Finney said, "God is like a great pent-up revival." He simply waits to release the pent-up flood when He hears someone crying out for revival.

You see, the heart of the Lord is so full. It is almost ready to burst with floods of revival upon this earth. If the cry of students through the centuries caused the Lord to open His heart upon college campuses in the past, how much more will your cry release His bursting floodtide today.

The cry of a fatherless generation has pierced His heart, and He only waits to hear *your* cry for revival. Then, just as He promised, He will come with the Holy Spirit and fire, setting your campus ablaze today and *America Ablaze* tomorrow.

Endnotes:

1. Yale College was founded in 1701 by Elihu Yale as a place where "youth may be instructed in the Arts and Sciences who through the blessing of Almighty God may be fit for employment both in the Church and Civil State" (quoted in Jay Rogers,

"Revival—Yale College," in *The Forerunner*. Internet: www.forerunner.com, 1990, p. 1). In Williamsburg, Virginia, James Blair wanted to establish a Christian college. King William and Queen Mary gave money to help support Blair's "project for souls." The expressed purpose of William and Mary College was to furnish a seminary for ministers of the Gospel as well as training youth in good manners (James E. Orr, *Campus Aflame: Dynamics of Student Religious Revolution* (Glendale, CA: Regal Books, 1971), p. 5.

The original colleges—Harvard, Yale, and William and Mary—were founded for the glory of Jesus Christ. And when the First Great Awakening broke across the eastern seaboard in the 1740s, new Christian schools—Princeton, Hampton-Sydney, Dartmouth, Brown, and others—sprang out of what James Edwin Orr called "the educational passion of the Great Awakening." Then came the American Revolution. In the wake of the Revolution, college students were intoxicated with independence, pride, and rugged individualism. Campuses became seedbeds for deism and atheism. Immorality, profanity, gambling, and persecution of Christians became common sport (James E. Orr, *Campus Aflame*, p. 13).

2. Quoted in C.L. Thompson's *Times of Refreshing: Being a History of American Revivals* (Rockford, IL: Golden Censer Company, 1877), p. 79.

3. Archibald Alexander had been saved at the age of seventeen through reading the writings of Puritan theologian John Flavel. Now he decided to visit Hampton-Sidney. Alexander later said that when he came to Hampton-Sidney, the experience was one of the most unforgettable in the whole of his life (James Alexander, *The Life of Archibald Alexander* [New York: Charles Scribner, 1854], pp. 55-56).

A few years later, a revival broke out at Yale under the leadership of Timothy Dwight, Jonathan Edwards' grandson. Princeton had experienced a transforming revival in 1815. The president, Ashbel Green, wrote that "the divine influence seemed to descend like the silent dew of Heaven" (Ashbel Green, "A Report to the Trustees of the College of New Jersey [Philadelphia: William Fry Printer, 1815]). I have skipped over these to focus primarily on the revivals that came because of the earnest prayers of students.

4. Clarence Shedd, *Two Centuries of Student Christian Movements* (New York: Association Press, 1934), p. 52.

5. At Harvard, when students were reprimanded for irreverence during chapel, a student shouted, "It's a damned lie!" (Samuel E. Morrison, *Three Centuries of Harvard* [Cambridge, MA: Harvard University Press, 1936], p. 185). At Princeton, a deck of cards fell out of a hole cut in a Bible. Chapel services across the country were interrupted with "profanity and sputum" (James E. Orr, *Campus Aflame*, p. 19).

6. Clarence Shedd, *Two Centuries*, pp. 132-133.

7. E. Stanley Jones, *Song of Ascents: A Spiritual Autobiography* (Nashville: Abingdon Press, 1968), p. 68.

8. E. Stanley Jones, *Song of Ascents*, p. 69. Jones told James E. Orr that the revival at Asbury prepared him for his call to the mission field. He became the best-known Methodist missionary to India in the twentieth century, but it all began in a little campus dorm room when the fire of revival ignited his heart and ultimately resulted in calling him into world evangelism and missions (J. Edwin Orr, *Campus Aflame*, p. 89).

9. As God breathed out His Spirit, small Bible studies suddenly mushroomed in attendance. Students met in small groups on campuses all over the nation to pray for God to send revival to their campus. Timothy Beougher wrote that the awakening eventually touched "virtually every campus in America" (Beougher,

"Student Awakenings in Historical Perspectives," in *Accounts of a Campus Revival, Wheaton College 1995* [Wheaton, Il.: Harold Shaw Publishers, 1995), p. 39.

10. *Life* magazine, "College Revival Becomes Confession Marathon," 1950, 28(8), p. 40.

11. Mary Dorsett, "Wheaton's Past Revivals," in *Accounts of a Campus Revival,* pp. 69-70.

After this, students fanned out across the nation and visited other campuses, telling their stories. Intense thirst burned in the hearts of college students everywhere, and they began crying out to God for revival on their campuses. "Soon, more than a score of college campuses were aflame with revival fire," wrote Fred W. Hoffman (Hoffman, *Revival Times in America* [Boston: W.A. Wilde Co., 1956], p. 165).

12. Henry C. James and Paul Rader, *Halls Aflame: An Account of the Spontaneous Revivals* (Wilmore, KY: Department of Evangelism, Asbury Theological Seminary, 1966), pp. 8-9.

The tide rose higher and higher in Hughes, lasting on through the week. The revival spread over to the seminary across the street, through the town of Wilmore, and throughout the nation. Everywhere Asbury students journeyed to tell their stories, the Spirit of God came in power.

13. Robert Coleman, *One Divine Moment* (Old Tappan, NJ: Fleming H. Revell Co., 1970), p. 27.

14. During that same year at Wheaton, groups of students desperately prayed for revival, especially after they had heard about the Asbury outpouring. Two hundred students crammed a small chapel where two Asbury students had been invited to speak. Painful and humiliating confession of sin, followed by sincere pleas for forgiveness came forth. One young man said, "I have never been in a place where the Spirit of God was so overpowering. It was like electricity going through the room." Henry Liginfelter described a similar response: "The Holy Spirit's presence was overpowering. Everybody was just bent over pews, praying and confessing. It didn't make any difference. Most of us were bowed so low we couldn't have got up if we'd wanted to" (quoted in Timothy Beougher, "Times of Refreshing: The Revival of 1970 at Southwestern Baptist Theological Seminary," in *Evangelism for a Changing World* [Wheaton, IL: Harold Shaw Publishers, 1995], p. 22).

15. David McKenna, *The Coming Great Awakening*, 1990, p. 59.

All through Church history, young men and women have been the most open, the most receptive, and the most profoundly impacted by revivals. Clarence Shedd, historian, observed: "In all ages, the great creative religious ideas have been the achievement of the intellectual and spiritual insight of young men. This is evidenced by such names as Jesus, St. Francis of Assisi, Savonarola, Loyola, Huss, Luther, Erasmus, Wesley, and Mott. ... Many of the most revolutionary ideas have been worked out by young men under thirty and frequently by youths between eighteen and twenty-five" (Clarence Shedd, *Two Centuries,* p. 1).

I would add that Evan Roberts was a student and only twenty-six years old when the Holy Spirit fell on him to lead Wales in a national revival that affected the whole world.

16. Edwards wrote, "There was a remarkable outpouring of the Spirit of God on the children of Israel in the wilderness, but chiefly on the younger generation ... , the generation that entered into Canaan with Joshua. ... But the old generation were passed by; they remained obstinate and stiff-necked, were always murmuring, and would not be convinced by all God's wondrous works that they beheld. ... Let the old generation in this land take warning from hence, and take heed that they do not refuse to be convinced by all God's wonders that he

works before their eyes, and that they do not continue for ever objecting, murmuring, and caviling against the work of God, lest while he is bringing his children into a land flowing with milk and honey, he should swear in his wrath, concerning them, that their carcasses shall fall in the wilderness" (Jonathan Edwards, *Some Thoughts Concerning the Present Revival of Religion in New England*, in *Works*, Vol. I [Edinburgh: Banner of Truth Trust, 1995], p. 423).

17. Told by Cindy Jacobs in a message at Brownsville Assembly of God, September 2000.

18. Chris Robeson, "Rend Your Hearts," in *Revival!* John Avant, Malcolm McDow, Alvin Reid, eds. (Nashville: Broadman and Holman Publishers, 1996), p. 37.

19. Henry Blackaby, "Foreword," in *Revival!* John Avant, Malcolm McDow, Alvin Reid, eds. (Nashville: Broadman and Holman Publishers, 1996), p. 160.

20. Quoted in Douglas Munton, "The Movement in Texas," in *Revival!* John Avant, Malcolm McDow, Alvin Reid, eds. (Nashville: Broadman and Holman Publishers, 1996), p. 95.

21. Timothy Beougher, "Revival at Wheaton College, in *Revival!* John Avant, Malcolm McDow, Alvin Reid, eds. (Nashville: Broadman and Holman Publishers, 1996), pp. 105-106.

22. Lyle Dorsett, "The Wheaton Revival of 1995: A Chronicle and Assessment," in *Accounts of a Campus Revival: Wheaton College 1995* [Wheaton, IL: Harold Shaw Publishers, 1995], pp. 82-83.

23. I was amazed at the results from the Brownsville students. In every category, their responses were by far the highest, revealing an incredible emphasis on holiness and repentance.

24. See the framework of this study and the questionnaire in the Appendix.

25. Wishard also helped organize a month-long camp for college students at Moody's Mount Hermon campgrounds. Out of this came a tremendous missions thrust. John R. Mott said that the Mount Hermon camp experience was "the spiritual center" of the missionary uprising which ultimately sent twenty thousand students into foreign missions in the early twentieth century (John R. Mott, *The Pastor and Modern Missions* [New York: Student Volunteer Movement for Missions, 1904], p. 95).

26. In those days, the YMCA was strongly evangelical.

27. The Chi Alpha website is www.ChiAlpha.com. The Brownsville Revival School of Ministry website is www.BRSM.org.

Ministering God's Love

The
Father-Wound

Humbly Washing Feet

Chapter 8

The Father-Wound

Slip with me for a moment back two millenniums, into an upper room in Jerusalem. Watch Jesus rise from a table and strip off His outer robe. See a mysterious smile curl His lips and warm tears gleam in His eyes. Look now as He reveals the glory of His humility.

See Him wrap a servant's towel around His waist, and watch Him as He humbly kneels and washes His disciples' dirty feet. Look on as the One who is clean washes those who are dirty. When He finishes, hear Him say, *"Now that I, your Lord and Teacher, have washed your feet, you also should wash one another's feet"* (John 13:14).

Now turn your thoughts forward two thousand years and edge your way into a crowd at The Call DC. Stand in awe as Coach Bill McCartney asks his son to sit in a chair before him. Then, in front of almost four hundred thousand people, see the coach kneel and wash his son's feet. As he washes, he prays, weeps, and asks forgiveness, his tears dripping down on the feet of his son. Then he kisses his son's feet, an act of deep humility and love. Not a dry eye can be found in the crowd.

Now see fathers all around you bend down and wash the feet of their own kids, weeping as they wash. See sons and fathers, daughters and dads embrace as years of hurt wash away and forgiveness flows like fountains.

Turning the Hearts

In the closing words of the Old Testament, the prophet Malachi said, *"He will turn the hearts of the fathers to the children, and the hearts of the children to their fathers"* (Malachi 4:6, NKJ). Without this turning of the hearts, the land, Malachi predicted, would be cursed.

This turning is *"a reconciliation produced by repentance,"* the Amplified Version reveals. That's why humbling ourselves in repentance to one another is a key to spreading the blessing of revival throughout our nation. I believe this is what God is waiting to see before He fully sets *America Ablaze.*

One night in our revival camp, before most of the students had gone home for the summer, we sat around a campfire, roasting hot dogs. Then suddenly, those men and women surrounded me and began washing my feet.

As they splashed water over my feet and prayed, the Holy Spirit gave me a word for them. He nudged me to say, "Now, you go home and wash your own parents' feet. Humble yourselves and watch the Lord heal the gaping wound between the generations."

Yours has been called the fatherless generation, primarily because so many of you have grown up without a dad in the home. Richard Crisco, who pastors hundreds of youth at Brownsville, says that children are desperate for a dad.[1] Jay Strack and Ron Luce, in their book *Turning the Hearts of the Fathers*, said, "Kids are hungry for a father."[2]

If ever there was a time when fathers and their children needed to have their relationships healed, it is now. *Time* magazine reports this about the American family:

> More children will go to sleep tonight in a fatherless home than ever in the nation's history. Talk to the experts in crime, drug abuse, depression, school failure, and they can all point to some study somewhere blaming those problems on the disappearance of fathers from the American family.[3]

Now I want to ask: What if—all over this wounded nation—young men and women started reaching out in love to their dads? What if you really forgave your dad for his mistakes? What if you stooped to wash his feet? What if you even asked him to forgive you?

What do you think God in Heaven would do if He saw the hearts of children turning to fathers and fathers to the children? I believe He would set *America Ablaze!*

The Love of a Dad

There's something I now want you to consider: No matter how it may look to you, your dad loves you, and he longs for a relationship with you.

Maybe your parents were split apart and you rarely, if ever, heard from your dad while you were a child.

Even so, I can tell you, he holds a deep ache in his heart for you. The older he gets, the more he yearns for a relationship with you. But the years have passed, and he probably doesn't know how to repair the breach.

That's why, if you could reach across the chasm to him, the relationship could be healed. This calls for courage and humility on your part, but it would please the heart of God to see it happen.

You may feel, however, that your dad should have been the one to reach out to you. This is true, but he bears hurts you may not know about. Part of his hurt could be a father-wound in him.

I want to talk to you now about this possibility of a father-wound in your dad, which may have kept him from knowing how to be a real father to you. This will help you better understand him. As one of our revival students told me, "Understanding my dad's father-wound gave me compassion for him. It helped me forgive him!"

Not only will understanding his father-wound give you compassion for your dad; it will help you see that the reason he seemed to reject you was not your fault. Ultimately, I believe, it will help turn the hearts of fathers and children back to each other, so America can be healed and ignited with revival.

The Father-Wound

In his book *Father and Son*, Gordon Dalbey explains, "I have discovered that inside every business suit, every pair of faded overalls, every stay-press sportshirt, lies the wounded heart of a boy longing for his daddy." He continues, "No pain strikes more deeply in the heart of a man than to be abandoned by his dad—either physically or emotionally." [4]

In his book *Loose That Man and Let Him Go!* T.D. Jakes says, "Our father's absence can form a sustained question in our minds, a haunting thought, *Maybe it was something I did or something I lacked that caused him to leave.*"[5] This thinking spawns a suppressed, but gnawing, guilt.

Because men often feel abandoned by their own fathers, they find it hard to know how to be relational with their own kids. What's more, they find it difficult to model manhood to their sons. Therefore, says Dalbey, "The vast majority of men in our society today are imprisoned and crippled by a condemning voice that tells us we do not measure up as men."[6]

Stephen Strang, author of *Old Man, New Man,* writes, "I have my own father-wound, and I've never known a man who didn't have one." Strang suggests that most men assume their children know they love them without their ever having told them so. "When it comes to a father's love," he says, "silence is crippling, not golden."[7]

The neglect of children, the sexual abuse of women, and even homosexuality can be traced to father-wounds. Dalbey says that most of the homosexual men to whom he has ministered "were molested or seriously abused as boys by older men—who thereby took advantage of that wound in the boy."[8] Strang notes the father void in the lives of young homosexuals. He relates these words of a young man:

> The inner pain started early in my life. At the age of 5, I promised my mother that I would care for her, in light of the abuse we all suffered from my father. But I craved attention from [other boys] to replace what was missing from my father.[9]

Dalbey explains, "Most men today long to feel secure in their manhood. But they are locked in, paralyzed by sin, overwhelmed by the loneliness of their father-wound and the emptiness of having been abandoned by their dads."[10]

Furthermore, says Dalbey, "Drugs, fear of women, job confusion, sexual immorality, suicide at a rate three times that of women, heart attacks—these and many other 'wolves' are devouring men today who are running from the father-wound."[11]

Richard Rohr tells the sad story of a nun who worked in a prison and was asked to order hundreds of Mother's Day cards for inmates to send to their moms. Then, as Father's Day approached, the nun thought she'd plan ahead this time and ordered crates of Father's Day cards. Years later, the nun told Rohr that not one inmate had requested a card for his father, and she still had the crates of unsigned and unsent Father's Day cards.[12]

Young man, young woman, do you see why it may have been so hard for your dad to relate to you? He may have had his own crippling father-wound and not have known how to show love, because he never saw it modeled. Now you may have to be like Jesus to him, humbling yourself, leading the way in love. If you will, I promise you this—Heaven will open over you. Even if your dad momentarily rejects your love, your heavenly Dad will smile down at your obedience.

What You Need to Hear

I ministered on this subject one night in my home church in Texas. I talked about the father-wounds in the young generation, as boys tried desperately to please their dads, but could never quite measure up. I talked about daughters, in search of a father's love, sometimes giving up their virginity in search of the love of a man—actually the love of their fathers. At the end of the message, I invited all those under thirty to come forward. I looked those young people in the eyes and sincerely repented to them for the pain we parents have inflicted on them from our divorces.

Then my former pastor, Glen Swartzendruber, came forward to speak to the kids and young adults. From the depths of his heart he said, "I want to stand in the gap as a father. I want to speak straight to your hearts and say—I am so very sorry. I was wrong. We were wrong. Will you forgive me?" They absolutely melted.

Then Pastor Glen slipped around to each one, hugging and praying for them individually. Into each one's ear he whispered something every son or daughter needs to hear: "I want you to know ... I am so proud of you!"

Pastor Glen was modeling what children of all ages

need from their dads. To show you what I mean, come for a moment down to the banks of the River Jordan.

Look now out over the water and see a rugged man, with trembling hands, slowly lowering the Son of God into the baptismal waters. Watch the heavens tear open and see the Father bless His Son with the Holy Spirit, then thunder down from above. The words the Father gave to the Son model for all fathers what every child longs to hear: *"You are My Beloved Son; in You I am well pleased"* (Mark 1:11, AMP). From that point on, the Son had the courage and the anointing to defeat the devil in the wilderness, walk on water, heal the sick, raise the dead, hang on a cross, and rise in resurrection power.

This is what Pastor Glen was modeling. He was saying to the young men and women of our church:

- I love you.
- I am pleased with you.
- I bless you with the Holy Spirit, as He anoints you for service.

You may never hear this from your dad, but I promise you this—if you will fully forgive your dad, you will hear it from your heavenly Father.

Forgiving Dad for Hurting Mom

Let me touch on another sensitive area. You may struggle with resentment, even rage, for the way your dad has treated your mom. You saw how hard she worked to keep the home together, but somehow she could never quite please her husband. After she had children and lost her teenage figure, your dad seemed to lose interest in her. You may have seen the pain she carried if he had an affair, or physically abused her, or drank too much, or mocked her commitment to Jesus.

Then, when the marriage ended, you saw how she felt numb, discarded, and terribly wounded. She received child support, but it wasn't nearly enough to support a family. She probably had to work, leaving you as part of the first group of latchkey kids in American history.

You may burn inside with anger because of what you saw, but consider this: Perhaps your dad's behavior was the result of his own paralyzing father-wound. Clinical psychologist Ken Druck links a man's dissatisfaction with his wife, as well as life in general, to the father-wound:

> I see many men walking around in mid-life with a sense of yearning for things that they can't get from their wives and can't get from their jobs and can't pull from inside themselves. Having listened to thousands of stories, ... I am convinced that what the men are missing is a sense of their own identity: a very primitive and very deep sense of validation that passes from fathers to sons.[13]

Do you see? Your dad may have been struggling to fill that masculine void in his life, but it had nothing to do with you or even your mom. I'm not excusing sin, but I'm trying to help you understand, so you can forgive your dad and let God heal your relationship.

Healing Father-Wounds

One day I gathered the revival students who live at our camp around the kitchen table and read them a preliminary version of this chapter. They sat riveted while I read, occasionally wiping away a tear or drips from their noses.

When I finished, they all agreed—this subject hit the center of the target, providing the answer they had been searching for as a fatherless generation. Each one began sharing around the table about his own father-wound.

One young man (I'll call him Joe) told how his dad had tried to be a good father, but sometimes he would explode with anger for no reason. The Lord told Joe to always honor his parents, keeping an attitude of love and respect. But still the wounds from his dad's occasional angry outbursts hurt him deeply. Furthermore, his dad had been unfaithful to his mom, and this was painful for the whole family.

Then Joe learned about the father-wound. He remembered that his dad's mom had died when he was very young. This had broken his grandfather's heart, and he had turned to alcohol, often mercilessly beating his son. Now Joe could understand why his own dad sometimes lost his temper. He could even understand why he had had an affair. Not that he approved of it, but he saw that his dad was searching to fill his masculine void. He needed his father-wound healed.

Now compassion filled Joe, and he could freely forgive his dad. Today, Joe's parents are healed and together in Jesus, which I genuinely believe is a result of Joe's compassionate prayers.

Another young man told me of his father's abuse of his mom and of several affairs his dad had. Although the marriage ended in divorce, the mom remained a deep and faithful Christian. It helped this young man to realize that the reason for his dad's infidelity was a hole in his soul concerning his masculine identity—in other words, a father-wound.

One story especially gripped us all. Ben's biological father had abandoned the family at his birth, causing him to feel there must be something wrong with him.

Years passed, and Ben's mom remarried. His new stepfather became his dad, and he loved him dearly. But when that marriage ended, too, the stepfather never again contacted Ben. He only reached out to Ben's half-brother, the biological son from the marriage. This bored the hole in Ben's heart even deeper. He was sure now that something *was* wrong with him.

Finally, Ben's real dad came back into his life, after nineteen years with no contact. When he invited Ben to come live with him, Ben gave up everything—his home, family, girlfriend, all that represented security—because he longed for the love of a dad. But, even then, his father would often fall into fits of rage, hitting him and making him feel worthless.

This sense of worthlessness still throbbed in Ben's heart when he came out to go to college at Brownsville Revival School of Ministry. Now, as we sat around the

143

table, Ben happened in on us and heard part of this chapter. As he listened, his wounds began to surface.

We all gathered around Ben and ministered to him for two hours. At one point, we invited Jesus into the memory of one of his most severe beatings. He recalled how he had always tried to respond with love, and suddenly he knew—Jesus was so pleased with him for that.

However, Ben still couldn't forgive himself for his father's abandonment. Though he wasn't at fault, that lie had lodged in his brain. So I held a hand mirror before his eyes and urged him to say to himself, "Ben, I forgive you." When he did this, freedom came. Now, the revival students prayed and the power of God came down. When we finished praying, he was so drunk with love and joy he could hardly talk.

Later he told me, "It was hearing about the father-wound that really helped me understand. It took the blame off myself and off my dad, too. You cannot imagine how different I feel. Everything has changed!"

The Wound in God's Heart

So what can be done about the father-wound? How can it be healed?

Once again, I call you to the feet of the Lamb. Turn your thoughts heavenward. With the eyes of your spirit, look up at Jesus. See Him on His throne, looking like a slain Lamb, still bearing marks from His sacrifice (see Revelation 5:6).

Now look closely at the lacerations on His chest and

shoulders, arms and legs. See His open hands still bearing punctures in the palms.

Keep looking. Focus the eyes of your spirit and see Him pull back the veil of His flesh. Now look as He bares His heart. Can you see it? Focus closely and you will see within His heart ... There it is—a gaping father-wound.

As we have seen, when the Father turned His face away and slammed His wrath down upon His Son, it tore a hole in Jesus' heart.[14] This is what wrenched from Him that horrific cry, *"My God, why have You forsaken Me?"* During Jesus' time of greatest need, the Father abandoned His Son, and just like yours, this tore Jesus' heart. Yes, your Jesus carries a father-wound!

But remember this—it's through that wound that a river flows out to you, and its soothing waters will heal the father-wound in your soul.

Yes, Jesus bore your father-wound in His heart. He did it so He could release to you Abba's river, the river teeming with life, and love, and the presence of God. So let it come. Let it flow. Sink your heart beneath those healing streams, and let His love flow in. Like a sponge in water, squeeze out all the grief buried so deep inside you. Let it out.

Weep in the river. Let the tears come up. Shamelessly cry out the pain from deeply embedded hurts with your dad. In the sweet presence of Jesus, weep out all the grief and pain ... until it all floats away in the currents of His love, like logs floating downstream in a river.

Now ask Him for His grace to forgive through you. Admit to Him that you are helpless to forgive, that you are powerless in this regard. Let His forgiveness come.

Breathe in deeply. Receive the power of the Holy Spirit to forgive. Then, forgive with all your heart—not in your power, but in His. Let His forgiveness flow through you to your dad.

But don't stop there. Put feet to your prayers. Write a letter. Make a phone call. Maybe even go and wash your father's feet. Let the forgiveness of Christ flow through you to him in practical ways. Humble yourself and ask him to forgive you for the ways you have hurt him. Let forgiveness flow like a fountain.

Regardless of your dad's reaction, now pause and look back up to the Lamb. Look up into the eyes of Jesus until you see it. There it is ... a drop of moisture forms in His eye and slides down His cheek. Hear the message in His tear: *You are My beloved child. I am so pleased with you!*

Let it come. Let His tears of love and approval splash down upon your heart. Receive His tears of acceptance and fatherly pride, letting them fill the hollow of your heart. Let the love of a heavenly Dad stream in, healing forever the father-wound in your soul.

Endnotes:

1. Crisco said that most fathers spend thirty-five seconds a day in meaningful conversation with their children. He points out that ninety-four percent of children who come from two-parent homes where they have healthy relationships with their parents, "especially dads," stay out of drugs, sex, and crime (Richard Crisco, in a sermon on Wednesday, October 18, 2000, at Brownsville Assembly of God, Pensacola, FL).
2. Strack and Luce said, "You'll never understand this generation's rebellion, resentment, restlessness, anger, aloofness, and distance until you understand this fact!" (Jay Strack and Ron Luce, *Turning the Hearts of the Fathers* [Tulsa, OK: Albury Publishing, 1999], p. 66).
3. *Time* magazine, June 28, 1993; quoted in Doug Stringer, *The Fatherless Generation* (Shippensburg, PA: Destiny Image, 1995), p. 16.

4. Gordon Dalbey, *Father and Son: The Wound, the Healing, the Call to Manhood* (Nashville: Thomas Nelson Publishers, 1992), p. 5.

5. T.D. Jakes, *Loose That Man and Let Him Go!* (Tulsa, Albury Press, 1995), p. 1.

6. Gordon Dalbey, *Father and Son*, p. 8.

7. Stephen Strang, *Old Man, New Man* (Lake Mary, FL: Creation House, 2000), pp 16-17.

8. Gordon Dalbey, *Father and Son*, p. 22.

9. *Exodus Update*, quoted in Strang, *Charisma*, September, 1999, pp. 91-92.

10. Gordon Dalbey, quoted in Strang, "When Father Wasn't There," *Charisma*, p. 90.

11. Gordon Dalbey, *Fathers and Sons*, p. 74.

12. Richard Rohr, "A Man's Approach to God," a tape series produced by St. Anthony Messenger Press, Cincinnati, OH, quoted in Gordon Dalbey, *Father and Son*, p. 7.

13. Ken Druck, quoted in Paul Ciotti, "How Fathers Figure," *Los Angeles Times Magazine*, June 18, 1989, p. 10; requoted in Dalbey, *Father and Son,* p.6.

14. Stephen Charnock, a Puritan theologian, said that, while Jesus bled upon a Cross, the Father "turned His smiling face from Him and thrust His sharp knife into His heart, which forced that terrible cry, '*My God, My God, why hast Thou forsaken Me?*' " (Stephen Charnock, quoted in Arthur W. Pink, *The Holiness of God* [Pensacola: Chapel Library, n.d.], n.p).

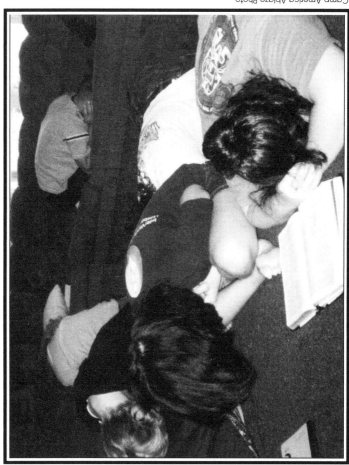

Broken at the Feet of the Lamb

Roaring Deep

Revival!

Chapter 9

Roaring Deep

Even now, as Jesus looks out over your generation, I believe He yearns to gush down tidal waves of glory. Already He has released streams of this coming glory, for the cry of the fatherless generation has pierced His heart.

And now, something has happened in our nation to prepare us for the massive floodtide. When news of the terrorists' attacks on our nation first came to the revival students at our camp, it had a marked effect on them. They didn't wait to listen to more news, and they didn't sit in shock watching television, as so many did. They burst out in prayer to God. They cried out with indescribable passion. They wept to Him in repentance and roared to Him for revival.

Our church and school at Brownsville had daily prayer meetings too, and on the Sunday morning following the tragedy, the service was incredible. After Pastor Kilpatrick gave an inspiring message on the godly history of America, he called us to stand in the gap and repent for the current sins of the nation. We had all been doing this for years, but somehow this was different. The whole church knelt and sobbed. We wept together for the sins of the nation. This was not done by just a few intercessors. Thousands of people wept and travailed in prayer for America.

A few nights later, Pastor Kilpatrick led the school in the most powerful outburst of corporate prayer I've ever experienced. Students, professors, staff, church members, and revival visitors walked through the church with tears bursting from their eyes, faces red with passion, and voices raised to the top of their lungs. They roared to God in groans of repentance and deep cries for revival.

I believe this is what is happening in churches all over this country as Christians cry out to God. We cry for the pain of the suffering in New York and Washington. We weep for the grief of the families. Most of all, we repent in godly sorrow for the sins of our nation, and we roar to Him for revival.

Thy Kingdom Come

Yes, the whole world is shaking. The foundations of America are trembling, but this is just what God said would happen:

> *Now he has promised, "Once more I will shake not only the earth but also the heavens." The words "once more" indicate the removing of what can be shaken—that is, created things—so that what cannot be shaken may remain. Therefore, since we are*

> *receiving a kingdom that cannot be shaken, let us be thankful, and so worship God acceptably with reverence and awe, for our "God is a consuming fire."* Hebrews 12:26-29

Though darkness covers the earth, the glory of the Lord will rise upon His Church (see Isaiah 60:2). And though the entire universe is quaking, it is so that *"the kingdom of the world"* will *"become the kingdom of our Lord and of his Christ, and he will reign for ever and ever"* (Revelation 11:15).

This is why we must pray. Jesus said to pray for His Kingdom to come and His will to be done on earth as it is in Heaven (see Matthew 6:9-10). We cannot take this for granted; we must pray. We must cry to God in prayer. We must roar in prayer for revival. If indeed revival is the breath of God, then revival will bring God's Kingdom to earth.

Today, the Lord is breathing on you, just as He breathed on His disciples in the Upper Room, and just as He roared His winds of the Spirit down at Pentecost. He breathes His holy wind and fire on you, so that you can go out and harvest the souls of America and the world. He calls your generation, with the older generation cheering you on, to go out and bring in the fruit of lost souls to the Kingdom.

The Coming World Revival

As Jesus draws closer to earth, the floods precede Him, for *"He will come like a pent-up flood that the breath of the* LORD *drives along"* (Isaiah 59:19). Nearer and nearer comes the floodtide. Can you hear the roar of the coursing waters?

It's like the native people who first discovered Niagara Falls. They heard the thunder of crashing waters in the distance, and the sound drew them. That's why they first named it *Onguiaahra*, meaning "Great Thunderer of Waters."[1]

Can you hear the thundering waters of global revival coming closer and closer? Can you smell the rain in the air? Already the thunder rumbles in the distance.

At Pentecost, great multitudes of Jewish representatives from many nations filled the city of Jerusalem, but only a few thousand listened to the wind and followed the tuggings of the Spirit to the Upper Room. In our day, millions have followed the heart drawings to upper rooms such as Toronto, Pensacola, Pasadena, and other revival wellheads. But sadly, millions more have missed the river. They've heard about the revival, but they've resisted the tuggings. Even as sunlight melts wax and hardens clay, the hearts of many are being revealed by the present outpourings of revival.

Jonathan Edwards looked ahead with visionary perspective and spoke of an extraordinary outpouring of revival which would come about in a latter day of glory. He wrote, "It is evident from the Scripture that there is yet remaining a great advancement ... of the Kingdom of Christ in this world, by an abundant outpouring of the Spirit of God, far greater and more extensive than ever yet has been."[2]

Edwards said that when, at last, the Holy Spirit comes

in this latter day of glory, we will see conversions beyond anything that has ever occurred in history. He was not promoting universalism, a heretical view, but he saw a universal spread of the Gospel in the promise of the Scriptures: *"The earth shall be full of the knowledge of the* LORD, *as the waters cover the sea"* (Isaiah 11:9, KJV).

Edwards compared this outpouring of revival to the streaming out of Ezekiel's river, which flows from the sanctuary, toward the east, running into the Dead Sea and healing its waters (see Ezekiel 47). He said this represented the "conversion of the world" to Jesus Christ in the latter days.[3]

Soon, Christ shall come as *"the Desire of all nations"* (Haggai 2:7, KJV), as all the earth looks to Him and is saved (see Isaiah 45:22). *"And the kingdom and dominion, and the greatness of the kingdom under the whole heaven, shall be given to ... the saints of the Most High"* (Daniel 7:27, KJV).[4]

Jonathan Edwards believed the Feast of Tabernacles[5] would be fulfilled by a grand worldwide revival.[6] He said that this feast was *"the glorious feast that God shall provide for all nations"* (Zechariah 14:17).[7] Those who do not attend this great outpouring of revival, he said, "shall have no share in the showers of divine blessing that shall then be poured out."[8]

He believed that this latter day of glory would be a time of great light and revelation and knowledge of God, which would increase through the earth as *"the kingdoms of this world are become the kingdoms of our Lord and of his Christ"* (Revelation 11:15, KJV). So great will be this outpouring of God's Spirit that this will indeed be a time of the Kingdom of Heaven on earth.[9]

World Christian leaders today are also foreseeing a massive global revival. In his book *The Rising Revival*, C. Peter Wagner wrote, "Our generation will soon experience such a vast global divine initiative that virtually no one will question whether it is true revival."[10]

Billy Graham spoke also of this coming worldwide revival. He said, "I believe as we approach the latter days and the coming of the Lord, it could be a time also of great revival ... showers falling from Heaven upon all the continents before the coming of the Lord."[11]

As I mentioned earlier, in 1994, three weeks into a forty-day fast, Bill Bright received a word from the Lord about this coming revival. He saw it sweeping "North America and much of the world," bringing in "the greatest spiritual harvest in the history of the Church."[12] Just as Bright predicted, that revival began before the year 2000 ended. The river fell especially on a young generation. That is why so many have overlooked it. But soon these underground rivers will converge and sweep the nation.

Can you imagine how glorious this will be, as Niagaras of revival break out across the land? Already I can hear the roaring floods. Can you hear the thundering of their waters? Can you feel your heart pounding faster? Does your face burn with the sunlight of God's glory coming closer and shining down upon you?

If God's glory caused lightnings and thunder and a whole mountain to shake in Moses' day, what will happen to the whole world as floods of His glory burst out more and more upon this earth, streaming from the pent-up heart of Christ? How much more will the ocean of glory, pouring from the Father-wound in the heart of

Jesus, cause the whole world to fill with glory, preparing the Bride for her King.

We all believe that Jesus is coming very soon, but He actually said that *"this gospel of the kingdom will be preached in the whole world as a testimony to all nations, and then the end will come"* (Matthew 24:14). The Greek word here translated *"nations"* is *ethnos*, meaning every ethnic group. Yet, in this world today, there are over a billion people who have never even heard of Jesus Christ.

Missiological reseacher David Barrett's best estimate is one billion six hundred thirty-seven million people have never heard about Jesus.[13] Jesus is coming soon, but first we have unfinished business to accomplish. This is why soul-winning is so uppermost in the heart of God today.

The Young Harvesters

Already, your young hearts are burning with fire and boiling at the presence of God, just as Isaiah said, *"as fire burns brushwood, as fire causes water to boil"* (Isaiah 64:2, NKJ). You've turned your backs on lukewarm religion. Your hearts leap and blaze with love for God. Your spirits burn with passion for souls. You are those who are going out—sent by the Lord—to reap the harvest of the fruit of nations.

I've watched thousands of young soul-winners right here in Pensacola literally champing at the bit to get out on the mission field or into the streets of the inner cities. They are like young calves ready to be released from the stall (see Malachi 4:2). These guys are passionate for souls. That's why, here in Pensacola, they hit the streets every weekend, pouring out their hearts to witness for Jesus.

Dipping every word in love, they urge sinners in front of clubs and on beaches to get right with God before it's too late. Their approach is blunt but filled with love and yearning. I watched one girl at the beach plead with a man to come back to Jesus, and the power of her words nearly knocked me over.

A passerby might see lost souls kneeling on the street in front of bars or liquor stores, weeping their way to Christ. Then, on Saturday night, students lead an evangelistic service in which street people and former alcoholics run to the altar to get saved.

Those conducting the services are the young harvesters who have been prepared in recent years for global revival. They are already exploding across the earth, carrying the Gospel of Christ to the more than a billion and a half people who have never heard of Jesus and His dying love for them.

Converging Rivers

In February 2001, a "Bridging the Americas" conference was held at Brownsville, and it was one of the most powerful conferences ever held here. It seemed to me that the reason so much power was being released was that three main worldwide tributaries of revival had come together: Toronto, Argentina, and Brownsville.

In chapel one morning at Brownsville Revival School of Ministry, I asked Toronto's John Arnot if he thought the three converging rivers had implications for world-wide revival. He called me forward, and before he could touch me, the Holy Spirit hit me. I jackknifed backwards but recovered enough to remain standing. John asked the Holy Spirit to meet my hunger, which he had felt in the question I asked. I don't think he ever did touch me, but the Holy Spirit knocked my feet out from under me, and I fell backward to the floor.

John and his wife Carol then went around praying for every student in the chapel. As students cried out, shook, and fell praising God in tears, I had the feeling that the pent-up heart of Jesus was finding release. For days, the Brownsville students were still manifesting the power of the Holy Spirit, even in classes.

However, this question about the converging rivers kept rolling around in my spirit. One night at our "Soak" meeting with revival college students, held weekly at our camp, the Holy Spirit showed me about the power of converging rivers. I saw a vision of the glory of the Lord bursting out from the heart of Jesus on the throne, pouring down in rivers to the earth.[14] Rivers were pouring into earthen vessels, and when people joined together—not separately, but together—this caused the converging of several rivers.

I realized that this is why prayer tunnels are so powerful. Like Niagara, when many rivers mingle together, this produces massive power—spilling, roaring, thundering over the cliffs of this world. It's like the psalmist said, *"[Roaring] deep calls to [roaring] deep at the thunder of Your waterspouts; all Your breakers and Your rolling waves have gone over me"* (Psalm 42:7, AMP).

But the Lord urged me to warn these students never to become "one-man rivers." The older movements in our country still have many such one-man rivers, but the Lord wants to merge and join the individual rivers until the waters converge in this coming worldwide revival. As rivers come together, like Niagara, the power multiplies, and the Holy Spirit's energy sweeps out to more and more people. This is how the whole earth will be filled with the glory of the Lord as the waters cover the seas.

What the Prayer Tunnel Represents

On another day in spring, at a chapel service, once again the students formed prayer tunnels. I stood back and watched, thinking, *This is indeed the converging of hundreds of rivers, now mingling together and flooding out in Niagaras of glory.*

The roof almost came off as students poured and roared and imparted the spirit of revival to one another. The heat of the fire caused faces to shine with the glory of Jesus. Students wept and wailed, burned and flamed with the spirit of revival.

After staggering through the prayer tunnel myself, I sat down and wrote:

> This is the most beautiful sight in the world: hundreds of students praying for one another as the presence of God floods the room. The Holy Spirit fans out across us all, for God Himself seems to smile. I watch students sobbing

with passion. They laugh and leap with happiness, exhilarated with joy. They worship and tremble in God's holy presence.

When I went through the prayer line a few moments ago, it was indescribable. Students plastered me with love, with anointing, with Heaven's holy fire. Now the Spirit of the Lord mounts, filling the sanctuary with the power of God. Young people stumble back to their seats, falling on their faces in prayer.

Never have I had such hope for America. If this kind of power from God can be released through so many nameless, faceless ones, even in the midst of the shaking of our nation, I know revival can sweep the land.

Yes, I am convinced that, with so many young men and women carrying the fire of revival, America can indeed be set ablaze. No one can resist this kind of joy and holiness, especially when it comes from our youth.

You young men and women are so open. Your hearts are not calloused by life. You are looking for something real. What could ring with greater authenticity than revival? What could be more genuine than the living presence of God? If the known world was turned upside down by the power of only a hundred and twenty from the Upper Room at Pentecost, how much more will a nation be ignited by hundreds and thousands in your generation, carrying the fire of revival!

As you move out, thundering in prayer and burning with passion, it will indeed be *"roaring deep"* crying passionately to *"roaring deep."* Then we will see a world set ablaze by the flames of global revival.

Roaring Deep From the Cross

Now, again, I want to ask you to consider the cry of Jesus from the cross. So, come once more to Jerusalem, to a hill outside the city. See the sun hide its face and the wind cease howling. Hear the breathless silence at Calvary, broken only by muffled groans and sobs.

Look up now at Jesus. Gaze with all your heart at your beloved Savior. ... There He hangs, blood draining from every wound in His body, fingers clawing the air, tongue swelling with thirst. See His eyes dripping with tears, blood vessels in His neck bulging. Watch flesh hanging in bloody shreds, the blood of God's Son spilling down arms and legs.

In the first three hours He spoke three times, but in these last three hours He has not spoken a word. He has not been able to, for He has been drinking His Father's cup.

Now, see Jesus suddenly push Himself down hard against the nail driven through His feet, filling His lungs with air. His eyes fly open wide. He looks up to Heaven, anguished tears swimming in His eyes, His face pale and stricken with horror. Then, suddenly, He bellows out through the universe—*"My God, why have You forsaken Me?"*

Did you hear it? Did you feel the *roar* in His cry? Puritan scholar John Flavel said it was like the "howl or roar of a lion," more like the "voice made by a wild beast than the voice of a man."[15] This is why scholars have often called this "the cry of dereliction."

In fact, when David forged those same words in Psalm 22:1, he screamed, *"My God, why have you forsaken me? Why are you so far from the words of my ROARING?"* The Hebrew root of the word translated *"roaring"* is *shâ'ag*, meaning "a rumbling, moaning, mighty roaring." Jesus roared the heart cry of the ages. It was *"roaring deep"* crying to *"roaring deep."*

That's why I believe He now waits to hear a roar from you, like an erupting volcano, expelling the hot molten lava of prayer from the hidden reaches of your inner-most being. I'm not talking about "animal noises." I'm talking about groaning, passionate, fervent, roaring prayer.

You are the young harvesters who will lead the way in revival. So let your cry meet His, as roaring deep cries to roaring deep ...

Roaring to God in repentance!

Roaring to God for lost souls!

Roaring to Him for another Great Awakening!

Roaring for healing between fathers and children!

Roaring for racial healing!

Roaring for the harvest!

Roaring to see *America Ablaze* with revival!

Roaring to God for floods of global revival!

From the very depths of your soul—roaring deep!

Endnotes:

1. Joan Colgan Stortz, designed by David Villavera, computer layout by Amy Morrison, *Niagara Falls* (Markham, Ontario: Irving Westorf and Co., Ltd., 1994), p. 2.

2. Jonathan Edwards, *An Humble Attempt to Promote Explicit Agreement and Visible Union of God's People in Extraordinary Prayer, and the Revival of Religion and the Advancement of Christ's Kingdom on Earth*, Vol. II, *The Works of Jonathan Edwards* (Edinburgh: Banner of Truth Trust, 1995), pp. 284-285.

3. Jonathan Edwards, *A History of the Work of Redemption*, Vol. I, *The Works of Jonathan Edwards* (Edinburgh: Banner of Truth Trust, 1995), p. 609. He wrote: "The time before this had been the church's sowing-time, wherein she sowed in tears and in blood; but now is her harvest, wherein she will come again rejoicing, bringing her sheaves with her. Now the time of travail of the woman clothed with the sun is at an end; now she hath brought forth her son: for this glorious setting up of the kingdom of Christ through the world, is what the church had been in travail for, with such terrible pangs for so many ages" (p. 609).

4. Jonathan Edwards, *The Works of Jonathan Edwards*, p. 609.

5. Jonathan Edwards said that Israel prepared for Tabernacles with the Feast of Trumpets and the Day of Atonement, which were a time of deep humiliation and repentance of sin. In the same way, the Church will be prepared for the fulfillment of Tabernacles by a time of humiliation and repentance. Yet God warned that those who do not attend this feast, which Edwards suggested refers to those who do not support the glorious outpouring of the latter-day revival, will have no rain upon their land. Edwards said, "They shall have no share in the shower of divine blessing that shall then be poured out" (Jonathan Edwards, *Some Thoughts Concerning the Revival of Religion in New England*, Vol. I, *The Works of Jonathan Edwards*, pp. 383-384).

6. Jonathan Edwards said, "This feast was on the seventh month of the year, which was a kind of holy sabbatical month, as the seventh day of the week was a holy day, and the seventh year a holy year, and also the year of Jubilee, at the end of seven times seven years. So this glorious state of the Church is to be in the seventh age of the world, or seventh thousand years" (Jonathan Edwards, *Notes on the Bible*, Vol. II, *The Works of Jonathan Edwards*, p. 775).
During this celebration, Israelites made booths of willow, palm, and olive branches. Edwards explains that the willow spoke of a flourishing Church, as a tree planted by streams of water; the palm spoke of a victorious Church, rooted and grounded in Christ; and the olive spoke of a Church filled with the Spirit of God.

7. For further study on the Feast of Tabernacles, see Leviticus 23:34-44, Deuteronomy 16:13-16 and 31:10-13, Ezra 3:4, Nehemiah 8:9-18, Zechariah 14:16-19, and John 7.

8. Jonathan Edwards, *Some Thoughts Concerning the Revival of Religion in New England*, Vol. I, *The Works of Jonathan Edwards*, pp. 384-385.

9. Edwards wrote: "The future promised advancement of the Kingdom of Christ is an event unspeakably happy and glorious. The Scriptures speak of it as a time wherein God and His Son Jesus Christ will be most eminently glorified on earth; a time, wherein God, who till then had dwelt between the cherubim—and concealed Himself in the Holy of Holies, in the secret of His Tabernacle, behind the veil, in the thick darkness—should openly shine forth, and all flesh should see His glory" (Jonathan Edwards, *An Humble Attempt*, Vol. II, *The Works of Jonathan Edwards* [Edinburgh: Banner of Truth Trust, 1995], p. 287).

10. C. Peter Wagner, "God Has Set His People A-Praying," in *The Rising Revival*, C. Peter Wagner and Pablos Deiros, eds. pp. 2-27 (Ventura: Renew Books, 1998), p. 9.

11. Billy Graham at the 1974 Lausanne Congress, cited in Graham, "The King Is Coming," in *Let the Earth Hear His Voice: International Congress on World Evangelization*, Lausanne, Switzerland, J.D. Douglas, ed. (Minneapolis: World Wide Publications, 1975), p. 1466. In his book *Storm Warning*, Graham predicted a time of world-shattering turbulence in every arena of life. He also envisioned a revival of hope that will prepare the whole world for the coming of Jesus Christ (Billy Graham, *Storm Warning* [Dallas: Word Publishing, 1994], pp. 309-313).

12. Bill Bright, *The Coming Revival: America's Call to Fast, Pray and "Seek God's Face"* (Orlando, FL: New Life Publications, 1995), pp. 35-36.

13. David B. Barrett and Todd M. Johnson, *International Bulletin of Missionary Research*, January 2001. (This number is provided by the world's leading missiological research team, headed by David B. Barrett. See www.gemwerc.org for more information).

14. In this vision, the whole earth was being bathed in the glory of God, and I instantly understood why Isaiah heard the seraphim crying, *"the whole earth is full of His glory!"* (Isaiah 6:3). The reason they speak of the earth as already being full of glory is because they live in eternity where there is no time and space. So from their perspective, the whole earth is already full of glory.

15. John Flavel wrote, "It was so sharp, so heavy an affliction to his soul, that it caused Him who was meek under all other sufferings as a lamb, to roar under this like a lion. ... Those words of Christ signify Psalm 22:1: *'My God, my God, why hast thou so far from the voice of my roaring?'* It comes from a root that signifies 'to howl, or roar as a lion; and rather signifies the noise made by a wild beast, than the voice of a man.

"And it is as much as if Christ had said, 'O my God, no words can express My anguish: I will not speak, but roar, howl out My complaint; pour it out in volleys of groans: I roar as a lion.' It is no small matter that will make that majestic creature to roar: and sure, so great a spirit as Christ's would not have roared under a slight burden. ... When they scourged, buffeted and smote Christ, He opened not His mouth; but when His Father hid His face from Him, then He cried out; yea, His voice was the voice of roaring; this was more to Him than a thousand crucifyings" (John Flavel, *The Works of John Flavel*, Vol. 1 [London: Banner of Truth Trust, 1968], pp. 41, 414).

Never the Same Again

A Revelation
of the Lamb
for America

"Take My Life, Lord Jesus!"

Chapter 10

A Revelation of the Lamb for America

September 11, 2001: The most devastating blow of terrorism in American history struck our nation. A few days later, I headed toward a chapel service at Brownsville Revival School of Ministry to pray.

As I drove, I thought about the interview I had just watched on a morning talk show. The hostess had asked one of America's leading evangelists, "If God is merciful, how could He allow so much suffering to come on this nation?"

The evangelist responded with a simple Gospel message, explaining that all have sinned and fallen short of the glory of God. He said that God gave His only Son on a cross so that we could be forgiven and cleansed of our sin.

As I listened, I felt like the words soared right over the heads of the commentators and probably over the heads of most non-Christians. What the man had said was good and true, but I felt something was missing.

As I knelt at the altar in chapel, the moment my knees hit the floor the Holy Spirit spoke to me. He said, "America needs a revelation of the Lamb!"

With the Spirit of God still on me, I poured out my heart in my systematic theology class. Later that day, as we joined the nation in praying for America at noon, I delivered my soul to the student body, urging them to go out from the school, giving America a revelation of the Lamb.

And now, in the final pages of this book, I want to pour out to you what the Lord showed me that day.

Look Up!

Jesus said that a time would come when there would be distress and trouble and anguish, *"Men swooning away or expiring with fear and dread and apprehension and expectation of the things that are coming on the world."* He said that *"[the very] powers of the heavens will be shaken and caused to totter."* But He continued, *"When these things begin to occur, LOOK UP AND LIFT UP YOUR HEADS, because your redemption (deliverance) is drawing near"* (Luke 21:26, 28, AMP).

With all that has happened in our nation, we must indeed look up and see a vision of the Lord. A.W. Tozer said, "To regain her lost power, the Church must see Heaven opened and have a transforming vision of God."[1]

So, young man or young woman reading these pages, I urge you now—*look up!* Look beyond the roof above you. Look higher than the skies. Look farther than the first and second heavens. Lift your eyes, and, as the Holy

Spirit Himself pulls back the veil, look into the third Heaven.

Look now with all your heart at the One seated upon the throne. See the bleeding Lamb, still carrying fresh wounds from His crucifixion. The reason He looks like a slain Lamb in Heaven (see Revelation 5) is that He's been sliced and cut, with thorns and whip and nails and spear, like a lamb for sacrifice.

This is what America needs to see. We need to see the Lamb. Our country has become jaded to the Gospel and hardened to the cross. One reason is that we who have told the story have done so much too mechanically. We haven't described the wounds, the blood, the pain, and most of all—the agony of Jesus upon drinking the Father's cup.

We've summed it all up with "Jesus died for your sins," and we haven't understood why people didn't fall to their knees immediately and get saved. If they did get saved, we didn't understand why their salvation seemed to be so shallow? They seemed to have no depth of commitment, and soon many turned back to sin. Why?

It is my conviction that we have been presenting a shallow Gospel. That's why America now needs a revelation of the Lamb.

A Graphic View of Jesus

Paul said, *"Before your very eyes Jesus Christ was clearly portrayed as crucified"* (Galatians 3:1). This word *"portrayed"* in the original Greek was *prographo*, meaning "to paint a vivid picture and lift it up as on a public placard." Paul was saying that when he preached, he painted a graphic picture of Jesus Christ crucified. As John R.W. Stott said, he turned people's ears into eyes.[2]

Young men and women—future preachers, evangelists, teachers, prophets, pastors, and missionaries—the Holy Spirit calls you, like Paul, to preach Christ crucified (see 1 Corinthians 2:2). Many have said you are the John the Baptist generation, preparing the way of the Lord, but what was John's highest calling? What was the most profound utterance that ever fell from his lips? Was it not: *"Behold! The Lamb of God who takes away the sin of the world"* (John 1:29, NKJ)?

John called a lost generation to behold the Lamb, and I believe that is what God is now calling you to do as well. As Charles Spurgeon said, "It is the preacher's principal business ... , his only business, to cry, 'Behold the Lamb of God!' "[3]

Our nation is shaken and broken right now, and Americans need to hear about Jesus, but please don't give them a simple, mechanical, memorized message. Former generations were persuaded by head knowledge, but postmodern generations must be touched at the core of their hearts.

So, show our people Jesus. Call them to behold the bleeding Lamb. Lift their eyes to Heaven. Cause their ears to become eyes as they see Jesus, bleeding and crying and roaring in agony as He drinks His Father's cup.

In this hour of dying hopes and shattering dreams, this is what we must have. All Americans must have a revelation of the Lamb!

Saved by Beholding the Lamb

One snowy Sunday morning in England, a fifteen-year-old boy made his way to a church in the village. A blizzard blew across the countryside, and snow and ice stung his eyes as he trudged on his way. Still, he was not deterred, for he was desperate. He wanted to find God, and he felt he must get to church to find Him.

As the boy blindly hurried through the snow, he realized he couldn't make it to the Baptist Church he had intended on reaching, so he stopped instead at a little Primitive Methodist Church which was nearer. He'd heard that these Primitive Methodists shouted so loud it would make your head ache, but in that moment he didn't care. He just wanted God. He slipped into the back pew and listened.

The regular preacher was snowbound that day, so an old man stood up to preach. He was uneducated, and spoke in crude country slang. He cried out, "The Bible says, *'Look unto me, and be ye saved, all the ends of the earth'* (Isaiah 45:22, KJV). So look! Look up now! See yer Savior bleedin' and dyin' upon a cross. See the blood drippin' down."

He spoke on: "Look up at Jesus! See Him risin' from the dead and ascendin' into Heaven. See Him sittin' down upon a throne."

Then the old man leaned over the pulpit and pointed straight at the fifteen-year-old boy on the back pew. He shouted, "Young man, you are miserable, and you will be miserable until you obey this Scripture—look unto Him and be saved!"

Suddenly, the boy's eyes opened, and he beheld the Lamb. In that moment, Charles H. Spurgeon was saved. It was a revelation of the Lamb that opened his eyes. That's why, for the rest of his life, Spurgeon preached the power of the cross of Christ.

"Calvary preaching, Calvary theology, Calvary books, Calvary sermons," said Spurgeon, "these are the things we want. And in proportion as we have Calvary exalted and Christ magnified, the Gospel is preached."[4]

Another time he cried, "Oh, down, down, down with everything else, but up, up, up with the cross of Christ!"[5] Charles Spurgeon had a revelation of the Lamb engraved upon his heart. He said:

> No subject is more sweet, more refreshing, more inspiring, more sanctifying to the saint than the cross of our dying Lord: the sinner needs it if he would be saved, but the saint requires it that he may persevere, advance, conquer, and attain perfection. Give me that harp and let my fingers never leave its strings, the harp whose strings resound the love of Christ alone.[6]

Once Spurgeon admitted that it was as though the cross had been burned on the back of his eyeballs. He said, "Paul knew nothing among the Corinthians save Jesus Christ and him crucified. ... In this respect some preachers know too much, and the sooner they join the holy know-nothings the better."[7]

Preach the Blood

It's like the missionary named Ruth who rushed up after I finished my brief message in chapel, in which I called the students to spread a revelation of the Lamb. She excitedly told me of being in a mall where two dark-skinned men tried to sell her some jewelry. One of them was a Hindu, and the other was a Muslim. She began sharing her faith with them both, and her words fell on deaf ears. That is, until she started telling them about the blood of Jesus. She described to them the wounds He suffered, the cross, the blood He shed that washes away sin.

Tears filled those men's eyes, and both of them prayed with her to receive the Lord. Later, one tried to pay her something. She graciously refused, telling him that what they had received was a free gift. "But you don't understand," he cried, thumping his chest with his hand, "I now have something inside of me!" It was a revelation of the Lamb that opened a sin-hardened man to the Gospel and made him grateful.

Steve Hill had a similar experience. He was preaching to a group of American young people. He told powerful stories of amazing conversions, but the more he preached, the more the kids chuckled and cut up. Several actually mocked the message.

Then the Lord said to him, "Preach the blood, Steve. If I be lifted up, I will draw all men unto Me. Speak of My suffering, My pain, My cross." Steve repented for grieving the Holy Spirit and began preaching about the pain and blood and crucifixion of Jesus. "Within just a few minutes, my listeners were weeping uncontrollably," he said. "The more I preached the cross, the more they cried. The altars overflowed. ... His sacrifice set them free."[8]

You see, your generation cannot be reached through the head; you must be reached through the heart. Doctrine, dogma, and intellectual arguments mean very little to you young postmodern men and women. Yours is a different generation today. Older people must come to understand that postmodernists relate through feelings, emotions, and experiences with God. That's why you can reach them with a gripping, graphic, heart-melting revelation of the Lamb.

Pierced by His Piercings

But before you can express the revelation, it must become real to you. "They preach Christ best who see him best," said Spurgeon.[9] You must see Jesus and be pierced by His piercings before others will be pierced.

So let's go again to Calvary and look up at Christ the Lamb. ... With the eyes of your heart, gaze on the wounds on His brow where thorns gouge His head like ice picks. Look at the blood trickling down His cheeks, mixing with tears and human spittle. See drops of blood and tears and saliva crusting in His beard.

See His hands and feet, bored through with iron spikes. See bright red streams of blood seeping from beneath the nails and dripping down His arms. See scarlet currents pooling under His feet and soaking into the ground below.

Look until you can see, really see. See the rips in His tattered chest and back and shoulders. See the mangled flesh hanging in ribbons from His body. See the deep, open gash in His side, pierced by the soldier's spear. See blood and water gush from His side.

This is what people need to see. They need to watch the red streams of blood flowing from the wounds of the Lamb until their hearts begin to tremble.

But don't stop there. Please don't leave the story before it ends.[10] Take the people deeper. First, however, *you* must take a deeper look.

See the sky turn as black as night as all nature hides its face from the scene before her. See darkness cover the Lamb, and see Him thrashing under the grotesque burden of the filth of human sin. See Him crushed for your iniquities, heaving and convulsing under the weight of your transgressions.

Look up at Jesus until your heart weeps with the reality of the sin He bore. For only then can you show America and all the nations what Jesus did for them. People need to look until they feel the magnitude of the horrible filth of their sin upon the Lord Jesus. They need to let it grip and squeeze their hearts until they fall to their knees and cry out to God for forgiveness.

There's still more, so much more. Look up into Heaven. Gaze beyond the cross and see into the heavenlies. Somehow, let the eyes of your spirit see the unthinkable. Let your heart stretch out to take hold of the meaning of it. Your mind won't be able to comprehend what I'm getting ready to say; only your heart can grasp the dimensions of this reality.

Look now into Heaven and see the Father holding a brass cup in His hand. The reason I think it is brass, not gold or silver, is because brass speaks of judgment.

Now see Him tip the cup. ... Watch Jesus turn pale. See His face blanch white as a sheet. See Him frozen in place, paralyzed by the gripping view before Him. Can you see Him there, like a pale and innocent lamb?

Now, watch the contents of the cup spill down. See the wrath of Almighty God roar down upon this Lamb. And see Jesus drink His Father's cup of infinite wrath.

Think about it. This is *infinite, eternal* wrath. That means Jesus endured the endless, limitless, everlasting wrath that had been rolled up, condensed, and compacted into three hours.[11] Furthermore, He endured the wrath *for all humankind*, compacted and poured down on one Man. Please pause and think about what this means.

Realize that Jesus took the full punishment of Hell upon himself—upon one Man in three hours of time. And during that time, He didn't just endure one man's Hell; He endured all of humanity's Hell.

See Him drink and drink and drink the cup of wrath ... until sin is completely demolished in Him. That's what the theological term *propitiation* means. I realize you may not like theological language, but this one is very important. It's really the hinge on which all theology swings.[12] It simply means, "a sacrifice to avert wrath." It means that Jesus took the wrath of God on Himself so it could be diverted from you.

Can you believe it? Oh, I tell you my heart has never ceased trembling since I learned that Jesus took God's wrath, so that it could be turned away from me. Nothing so burns me with passion, consumes me with a desire to tell others about Jesus, grips me with a burden for souls, and fills me with a vision for revival.

I want your heart to tremble with this passion for the Lamb, too. Nothing will keep you solid and stable and secure in your faith like a deep, gripping grasp of the cross. If your heart and life are forever fastened to the cross, as the nation shakes, you won't falter. You'll be able to stand.

Not only that, but your motives will burn and blaze with pure devotion to the Lamb. He will be the purpose for everything you do.

Now do you understand why Jesus cried that horrific cry from the cross, that cry of dereliction? It was the saddest cry ever heard upon this earth. I have mentioned it several times in this book because it is the same cry many of you have cried in the deep of night, as you drenched your sheets with tears. The cry is: "My God, why have You forsaken me?"

This is the cry that caused the earth to shake and the seas to roar. It's the cry that caused boulders to burst, rocks to crack. It's the cry that split the Father's heart and tore the veil in the Temple in two. It's the cry that destroyed the divide between Jews and Gentiles.

Most of all, this is the cry of your generation—the cry of abandonment. But it's the cry that broke open the heart of the Son and released a river of God's Spirit to a whole generation. It made it possible for the crack in your heart to fill with living water and the burning blaze of revival.

The Lamb Upon the Throne

But we still haven't finished the story. Come, look up again at Jesus. This time see Him seated as the Risen Lamb upon the throne, *"looking as if [He] had been slain"* (Revelation 5:6). That's why angels, seraphs, and elders cry, *"Worthy is the Lamb!"* (verse 12). Why is He worthy? They sing, *"You were slain and with your blood you purchased men for God"* (verse 9).

Look closely at this lovely Lamb, the Wounded Man upon the throne. Though a crown of gold rings His head, He still bears pierce marks from the thorns which once stuck His brow. Now, out of these piercings in His head, flow light beams of glory, causing His face to shine like the sun, His eyes to blaze like flames of fire, and His head and His hair to glow white as snow (see Revelation 1:14).

Look at His hands and feet. Though He holds a golden scepter, nail holes still carve His hands and feet. Now rays of glory stream out of His hands, for *"His brightness was like the sunlight; rays streamed from His hand, and there [in the sunlike splendor] was the hiding place of His power"* (Habakkuk 3:4, AMP).

Look now at His side. Though He wears a robe of majesty, His side is gouged from the blade of the spear. But look more closely, for out of this gaping wound flow currents of splendor. That's why the Lamb is the lamp of all Heaven. He radiates with the shekinah of God, for He is *"the sole expression of the glory of God [the Light-being, the out-raying or radiance of the divine]"* (Hebrews 1:3, AMP).

180

Now, draw up a little nearer and look into His eyes. See the tears of love and mercy gleaming there. Tune the ears of your spirit to hear His voice. Like the sound of Niagara Falls, He speaks, His words rushing like the thunder of many waters.

What does He say? I believe He calls you to go and cry in the wilderness of a shaking world: "Behold the Lamb of God!" If indeed you are the John the Baptist generation, then you are called to bring a revelation of the Lamb to America.

That's why America shakes. That's why the world totters and erupts with war. God calls people everywhere, from every tribe and tongue and nation, to look up and behold His Lamb.

The Most Precious Wound

As you close these pages, I ask you to lift up your eyes one last time. Look up to the Lamb upon the throne. Look beyond the wounds in His outer flesh and see the wound in His heart.

Many wounds sliced the flesh of your Savior— wounds in His hands, His feet, His back, His chest, His brow, and His side. But the most priceless wound of all is the Father-wound in His heart. That wound pulses with tenderness, holding back a river like a fragile dam holds back a surging river at floodtide.

Now your cry has pierced that wound and released upon you the eternal river of God. Floods and floods and more floods of liquid glory are already pouring out from the heart of the Lamb, tumbling down to earth. Can you hear the sound of it? Can you feel it? It comes closer as you draw near to Him. So come ... Draw up close to the Lamb—the Fountainhead Himself—and worship. In the words of Chris Dupree's powerful love song:

> *Romance me, O Lover of my soul,*
> *To the Song of all Songs.*
> *Dance with me, O Lover of my soul,*
> *To the Song of all Songs.*

Express your love to Him until He bends low and kisses your heart with His love. Let Him pour out on you His divine love, as you dance with the Bridegroom Himself.

And as His presence surrounds you, drink from the river of the Wounded Lamb of God. Soak your heart in the streams of delight. Drink up all the goodness of God. Let His new wine of joy fill every pore of your being. Let the glory of Christ saturate every cell of your being.

Let Him fill and fill and fill you until you can hold no more, and it must pour out through you—through the father-wound in your heart.

Let it flow. Let the rivers of living water burst out of your innermost being.

Let the spirit of revival burn through your prayers.

Let it flame through your words.

Let it glow from your face.

Let it stream through your tears.

Let it love through your life.

Let it issue through you to this nation, showing America a revelation of the Lamb.

Yes, let God use you—a fatherless generation—to fill this country and all the world with the glory of His presence. For you are the revival generation, handpicked by God, before the creation of the world, to set *America Ablaze.*

Endnotes:

1. A.W. Tozer, *The Knowledge of the Holy* (San Francisco: Harper & Row, Publishers, 1961), p. 121.
2. John R. W. Stott, *The Cross of Christ* (Grand Rapids, MI: Baker Book House, 1989), p. 343.
3. Spurgeon said, "It is the preacher's principal business, I think I might say, his only business, to cry, 'Behold the Lamb of God!' For this reason was John born and sent into the world, and such were the prophecies that went before concerning him. If he had been the most eloquent preacher of repentance, if he had been the most earnest declaimer against the sins of the times, he would, nevertheless, have missed his life-work, if he had forgotten to say, 'Behold the Lamb of God' " (Charles H. Spurgeon, "Behold the Lamb," in *Spurgeon's Expository Encyclopedia,* Vol. III [Grand Rapids, MI: Baker Book House, 1977], p. 103.
4. Charles H. Spurgeon, *2200 Quotations from the Writings of Charles H. Spurgeon*, Tom Carter, comp. (Grand Rapids, MI: Baker Book House, 1988), p. 46.
5. Charles H. Spurgeon, *2200 Quotations from the Writings of Charles H. Spurgeon*, p. 46.
6. Charles Spurgeon, "Behold the Lamb," in *Expository Encyclopedia,* Vol. III, p. 105.
7. Charles Spurgeon, "Behold the Lamb," in *Expository Encyclopedia,* Vol. III, p. 105.
8. Stephen Hill, *Time to Weep* (Orlando: Creation House, 1997), p. 48.
9. Charles Spurgeon, "Behold the Lamb," in *Expository Encyclopedia,* Vol. III, p. 104.
10. I cannot express the full extent of His sufferings in this brief chapter, but if you want more, see my book *The Masterpiece* or my upcoming book, *The Cry of the Fatherless Generation.*
11. I believe He endured wrath from noon, when the sky turned black, until three o'clock that afternoon, when He cried His last cry.
12. *Theology* is simply the study of God, and it's not a boring study. I think it's the most thrilling, faith-building, fire-burning study possible because it looks deeply into God. Of course, I would feel this way because I teach systematic theology at Brownsville Revival School of Ministry.

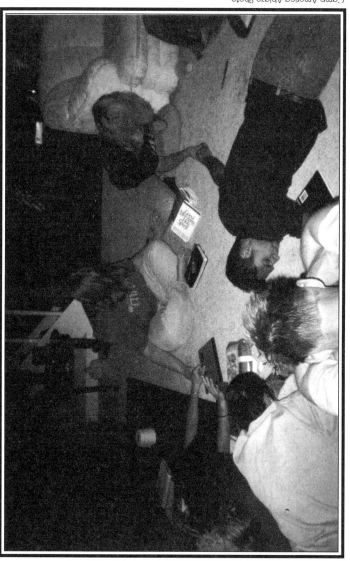

Spending Time in God's Presence

Appendix

The matrix on the following pages gives the framework of a questionnaire I sent out to college students across the nation who had experienced revival in 1995. The matrix is based on the marks of revival from three major revivalists: Charles Finney, Jonathan Edwards, and John Wesley. It measures the affective *(emotional)*, cognitive *(mental)*, and behavioral *(actual change)* responses to revival.

The number in the upper left corner, beginning with "2," corresponds to the number on the questionnaire. Question "1" asks if the young person believes this is a true work of the Spirit of God. This question stands alone and is not included in the matrix.

POSTMODERN REVIVALS	AFFECTIVE (Feelings/Emotions)	COGNITIVE (Knowledge)	BEHAVIORAL (Action)

Charles Finney's "Burning Conviction"

	AFFECTIVE	COGNITIVE	BEHAVIORAL
Confession of Sin	2. They *feel* convicted of sin and need to confess.	3. They *understand* the need to confess.	4. They *confessed* their sin to God and to others.
Repentance	5. They *feel* godly grief and sorrow for sin.	6. They *decide* to turn from that sin.	7. They *turned away* from sin.
Restitution/ Reconciliation	8. They *feel* sorrow over relationships.	9. They *decide* they will reconcile.	10. They *went* and *asked* forgiveness.
Love for Souls	11. They *feel* a new love for lost souls.	12. They *decide* to witness to the lost.	13. They *witnessed* to lost people.

Jonathan Edwards' "Distinguishing Marks"

	AFFECTIVE	COGNITIVE	BEHAVIORAL
Testifies to a deeper love for God	14. They *experience* God's presence more strongly.	15. They *understand* more about God.	16. They *fellowshipped* more with God.
Testifies to exaltation of Christ	17. They *experience* a deeper love for Jesus.	18. They *understand* more about Jesus.	19. They *exalted* Christ in worship and in life.
Evidences more love for others	20. They *feel* deeper love for brothers and sisters.	21. They *decide* to build more Christian relationships.	22. They *worked* on building relationships with others.
Evidences a love for the Bible and truth	23. They *experience* a deeper love for the truth of the Bible.	24. They *decide* to study the Bible more.	25. They *spent* more time in Bible study and walking in truth.
Evidences a love for the world	26. They *feel* less desire for worldly pleasures.	27. They *decide* to stop activities that do not honor Jesus Christ.	28. They *stopped* drinking, premarital sex, and smoking, etc.

John Wesley's "Fruit of the Spirit"

	AFFECTIVE	COGNITIVE	BEHAVIORAL
The fruit of the Spirit	29. They *feel* more peace, joy, and love.	30. They *decide* to walk in the fruit of the Spirit.	31. They *showed* more love, joy, and peace.
Attends small groups, chapel, or church	32. They *desire* to attend more Christian services.	33. They *decide* to attend more Christian services.	34. They *attended* more services.
Testifies to more time in prayer	35. They *desire* to pray and intercede more.	36. They *decide* to pray more.	37. They *spent* more time in prayer.
Commits to the ministry	38. They *feel* God's call to Christian service.	39. They *decide* to obey God's call to service.	40. They *committed* to God's call.
Social results	41. They *feel* a desire to help hurting people.	42. They *determine* to help with a social problem.	43. They *reached* out to help in a social need.

No._____

Gender: F___(1) M____(2)

Your age at the time of the revival____

Was this a campus____ (1); a church___ (2) Campus or church_____

The purpose of this survey is to analyze revival/renewal among those born from 1901-1981. There are no trick questions. Please check the line which best fits your response:

Yes|Not Sure|No

1. I believe the revival I experienced was a true work of God's Spirit.   ___ ___ ___

2. During the revival, I was deeply convicted of my own sin.   ___ ___ ___

3. I understood the need to make a public confession of my sin.   ___ ___ ___

4. I actually did confess my sin to at least one other person.   ___ ___ ___

5. I felt true godly grief and sorrow about my sin.   ___ ___ ___

6. I made a conscious decision to turn away from my sin.   ___ ___ ___

7. I have turned completely from my sin.   ___ ___ ___

8. I was deeply convicted over a broken relationship(s) in my life.   ___ ___ ___

9. I decided I would try to reconcile with the person(s).   ___ ___ ___

10. I went to the person(s) and asked forgiveness.   ___ ___ ___

11. After the revival, I began to feel a new love for lost souls.   ___ ___ ___

12. I have decided to start witnessing about Jesus to someone who is lost.   ___ ___ ___

13. I have actually begun to tell at least one person about Jesus.   ___ ___ ___

14. I felt God's presence very strongly during the revival.   ___ ___ ___

15. I think I understand more about God since the revival.   ___ ___ ___

16. I now try to spend more time in intimate fellowship with God.   ___ ___ ___

17. Since the revival, I feel a much stronger love and passion for Christ.   ___ ___ ___

18. Since the revival, I understand more about Jesus and His nature.   ___ ___ ___

19. I now try to more highly exalt Jesus in my worship and my whole life.   ___ ___ ___

20. I now feel a deeper sense of love for my brothers and sisters in Christ.   ___ ___ ___

21. I have decided to start building more and deeper Christian relationships. ___ ___ ___

22. I am now cultivating the deeper Christian friendships I decided to build.___ ___ ___

23. I now have an even deeper love for God's Word and His Truth. ___ ___ ___

24. I have made a decision to start spending more quality time in the Bible.___ ___ ___

25. I now spend more quality time in the Bible and walking in God's Truth.___ ___ ___

26. Since the revival, I feel less desire for worldly pleasures such as
drinking, smoking, and sex before marriage. ___ ___ ___

27. I have decided to cut back even more on some of the worldly
pleasures I practiced before the revival. ___ ___ ___

28. I have actually stopped certain worldly pleasures I used to practice. ___ ___ ___

29. I feel even more peace, joy and love in my heart since the revival. ___ ___ ___

30. I have made a decision to allow the Holy Spirit to cultivate even more
peace and joy and love in my life. ___ ___ ___

31. I think I am demonstrating even more fruit of the Spirit in my life. ___ ___ ___

32. I feel a desire to attend more small groups or chapel or church services.___ ___ ___

33. I have made a decision to go to more small groups, chapel, or church. ___ ___ ___

34. Since the revival, I have actually been attending more small groups,
chapel, or church services. ___ ___ ___

35. I have felt the need to spend more quality time in prayer and
intercession since the revival. ___ ___ ___

36. I have decided I will spend more time in prayer and intercession. ___ ___ ___

37. Since the revival, I now spend even more time in prayer. ___ ___ ___

38. During or since the revival, I have felt the Holy Spirit drawing me into
more Christian service or some kind of mission or ministry endeavor. ___ ___ ___

39. I have made a decision to obey God's calling into deeper areas of
Christian service, ministry, or mission. ___ ___ ___

40. I have answered God's call for service, mission, or ministry. ___ ___ ___

41. I feel a deep desire to be involved in ministry to others such as helping
the poor, reconciling racial problems, or winning the lost. ___ ___ ___

42. I have decided to get involved in helping to make this a better world. ___ ___ ___

43. I have started reaching out to help the poor, hurting, or lost people. ___ ___ ___

Analysis of the Results of the Survey

	All groups	Females	Males
1. Believed it was a true revival	86.67%	86.67%	86.67%

Charles Finney's "Burning Conviction"

	All groups	Females	Males
2. Felt conviction over sin *(affective)*	79.4%	84.4%	73.1%
3. Understood confession of sin *(cognitive)*	64.9%	68%	62%
4. Confessed sin *(behavioral)*	81.4%	84.5%	78.9%
5. Felt deep repentance *(affective)*	80.98%	81.9%	78.76%
6. Decided to repent *(cognitive)*	80.9%	83.88%	92.57%
7. Turned from sin *(behavioral)*	44.8%	49.77%	40.76%
8. Felt convicted of broken relationship/s *(affective)*	46.67%	64.58%	29.8%
9. Decided to make restitution *(cognitive)*	44.7%	58%	33.56%
10. Made restitution *(behavioral)*	42.58%	50.4%	37.98%
11. Felt passion for souls *(affective)*	64.8%	61.08%	67.4%
12. Decided to witness to others *(cognitive)*	62.18%	56.6%	65.6%
13. Witnessed to at least one other person *(behavioral)*	63%	50.3%	76%

Edwards' "Distinguishing Marks"

	All groups	Females	Males
14. Experienced the presence of God *(affective)*	87.38%	92%	82.1%
15. Understood more about God *(behavioral)*	88.19%	89.1%	88.3%
16. Had greater fellowship with God *(behavioral)*	82.72%	82.5%	83.2%
17. Had more love for Jesus *(affective)*	83.2%	81.59%	85.5%
18. Knew more of Jesus *(cognitive)*	83.1%	80.84%	85.71%
19. Exalted Jesus more *(behavioral)*	86.69%	83.75%	88.88%
20. Felt more love for others *(affective)*	85.82%	85.1%	87.38%
21. Decided to build relationships *(cognitive)*	81.15%	82.08%	81.38%
22. Built relationships *(behavioral)*	78.36%	78.87%	79.3%

23. Had more love for the Bible *(affective)*	89%	86.25%	91.96%
24. Decided to read the Bible more *(cognitive)*	81.23%	81.37%	81.28%
25. Read the Bible more *(behavioral)*	67.91%	63.99%	70.98%
26. Desired less of the world *(affective)*	57.7%	55.37%	58.65%
27. Decided to practice less worldliness *(cognitive)*	58.95%	50.37%	68.28%
28. Turned from worldiness *(behavioral)*	60%	59%	62%

John Wesley's "Fruit of the Spirit"

29. Felt more fruit of the Spirit *(affective)*	77.9%	72%	84.3%
30. Decided to demonstrate more fruit *(cognitive)*	86.81%	82.5%	90.4%
31. Demonstrated more fruit *(behavioral)*	68.8%	66.19%	67.7%
32. Desired to attend more services *(affective)*	65.3%	75.5%	75.5%
33. Decided to attend more services *(cognitive)*	66.98%	73.7%	61.4%
34. Attended more services *(behavioral)*	71.18%	72.2%	71.09%
35. Felt a greater desire for prayer *(affective)*	84.67%	83.46%	86.56%
36. Decide to pray more *(cognitive)*	73.34%	74.12%	72.12%
37. Prayed more *(behavioral)*	63.21%	59.4%	69.78%
38. Felt God's call to service *(affective)*	70.26%	66.3%	71.45%
39. Decided to obey God's call to service *(cognitive)*	80.9%	79.7%	81.99%
40. Answered God's call to service *(behavioral)*	74.97%	69.22%	80.8%
41. Desired to help the poor (affective)	79.75%	77.45%	82.56%
42. Decided to help the poor (cognitive)	84.4%	88.56%	82.13%
43. Helped the poor (behavioral)	81.06%	80.82%	80.26%

Youth Pastors: Bring your youth group to camp
and see them ignited with revival fire!

$25 a person per night

*"God set my youth group on fire for Jesus at Camp America Ablaze.
When they got home, they imparted revival to the whole church and
the fire still burns!"* — Youth Pastor Daniel Hewett

Tennis, swimming, sand volleyball, basketball, soccer, softball, prayer
garden, and use of kitchen facilities for meal prep

Thursday, Friday and Sunday morning at Brownsville Revival
Daily impartations from revival students

Call 334-962-7172
Website: www.revivalcamp.com

Dr. Sandy Kirk
Camp Director

College students, see our website for minimal cost and dates

for *"Spring Break Ablaze"* and *"Summer Break Ablaze"*